FINDING FAME

THE INSIDER'S GUIDE TO REAL
ENTERTAINMENT INDUSTRY CONNECTION$

MICHAEL FOMKIN
THE CONNECTION KING
VIP IGNITE / TALENT MANAGEMENT

MVHL

For permission requests, write to the publisher, addressed "Attention: Permissions Coordinator" carol@markvictorhansenlibrary.com

Quantity sales special discounts are available on quantity purchases by corporations, associations, and others. For details, contact the publisher at carol@markvictorhansenlibrary.com

Orders by U.S. trade bookstores and wholesalers. Email: carol@markvictorhansenlibrary.com

Cover Design - Low & Joe Creative, Brea, CA 92821
Book Layout - DBree, StoneBear Design

Manufactured and printed in the United States of America distributed globally by markvictorhansenlibrary.com

MVHL

New York | Los Angeles | London | Sydney

ISBN: 979-8-88581-113-2 Hardback
ISBN: 979-8-88581-114-9 Paperback
ISBN: 979-8-88581-115-6 eBook
Library of Congress Control Number: 2023916140

FOR YOUR FREE ONLINE AUDITION TO PUT INTO ACTION THE INCREDIBLE CONTENT IN THIS BOOK, WHILE AVAILABLE, PLEASE VISIT: HTTPS://VIPIGNITELIVE.COM/

VIPIGNITELIVE - HOW TO START YOUR MODELING AND ACTING CAREER

DEDICATION

To my mom, Philomena Fomkin.

Thank you for being my first fan and always seeing the best in me, even when I couldn't.

Your hard work and dedication as a single parent transformed me into the man I am today.

When things get hard and I want to quit, I think of you and rise to the occasion.

Thank you, Mom, for everything.

Your loving spirit will always be with me.

A VERY SPECIAL THANKS

I'd like to thank Marjah Simon.

You are my friend and sister. You mean more to me than anyone else in this life. You have been there as my guide—my mentor—who helped me overcome obstacles to find *belief* within myself. You see things in me that I could never see and have helped me reach levels of success that many dream about, and so few achieve.

Your wisdom, advice, and guidance have helped me become the best person I can ever be. So, this comes straight from the heart. Thank you.

ACKNOWLEDGMENTS

To **Deneen White**—Some people come into our lives for a reason, a season, or a lifetime; you came into my life at the right time for a lifetime. You are an inspiration, not only to me, but to everyone whose life you touch.
Reach for the stars and believe in yourself.

To **Alycia Kaback**—You set the standard for VIP Ignite and the Truth Management Team. Right from the beginning, you were on board with my vision and believed in my crazy schemes.

To the Wizard, **Robert Galinsky**—You are beyond amazing, and we attribute VIP Ignite to the incredible connections you created.

To our "Fairy Godmother of Broadway," **Pat Addiss**— It was you who helped us win the Tony.

To **Mark Schoenfeld**, the Pitchman of Hollywood— You are all the evidence someone needs to see that fortune favors the bold. Thank you for being the Gandalf Guide in our lives.

To **Ryan Colby**—Everything we know about fashion and running an agency came out of your brilliance.
I'm so glad you called me back.

To **Tony Robbins**—Thank you for creating the world of Platinum Partners. I had a life but didn't see it until you opened my eyes to who I really am. My whole life changed when I became a Platinum Partner.

SPECIAL THANKS

Thank you to the following contributors who took the time to share their insights, stories, and wisdom on the importance of connections in their entertainment industry journey. I urge each and every reader to look up these remarkable, talented people. Below, you'll see why these *real industry connections* mean so much to me.

Follow their magnificent careers to see what's possible when you are implementing what VIP Ignite and Talent Management teaches: learning how to make and nurture the right relationships will bring riches to your career, and true richness to your life.

Haviland Stillwell, Multi Hyphenate Actress, Singer, Producer, Director, Writer

I connected with Haviland through Alycia, who had invited her to be a part of her CBS radio show. When Alycia and I started working together, she introduced me to Haviland. She now comes to speak at our events and is one of the coaches for our talent.

Jessica DiGiovanni, Actress, TV Actress, Broadway Actress, Voice-Actress, Model

When I first spoke with Jessica, she was brand new to the industry. She accelerated tremendously and is now starring in another show on Broadway.

Jam Murphy, Wilhelmina Model, Actress

I met Jam about a year ago on set while filming for *Target;* she was really fun to work with in the movie. It was her first leading role in a feature film. There will likely be more leading roles as she continues in her career.

Santino Fontana, Tony Award Winning Actor, Voice of Prince Hans (*Frozen,* 2013), Voice-Actor, TV Actor, Broadway Actor

He was introduced to me about 15 years ago by Pat Addiss. He was early on in his career, but when he came to speak at our events, I could see his brilliance. We've been friends ever since.

Alexandria De Rossi, The Firm LA Model & Talent Agent

Ryan was the first one to connect with Alexandria, placing models with her agency. Later, she connected with Deneen, and we reached out to her to speak at our VIP Ignite events. And that is what this business is really about: connecting the dots.

Les Brown, Motivational Speaker, Politician, Former Ohio State Representative

Alycia was the one to connect me with Les Brown. She was the one who made it happen, and our relationship has only grown since.

Robert Funaro, *The Sopranos* (2001-2006), Actor, TV Actor

Robert has dabbled in every part of the industry—from TV commercials to series and films. He has worked with some of the industry greats. He appeared as Eugene on *The Sopranos* and co-starred with Denzel Washington in *American Gangster*. He is such a great person and one of our best coaches.

Thomas G. Waites, Producer, Director, Writer

He has over 40 years of experience in the industry, from acting to directing and producing, and is a really inspirational guy.

The Warriors was my favorite film as a kid. I was such a big fan. My whole life it was something that was always there in the background. About a decade ago now, I saw they were hosting a Warriors' convention. A lot of the guys from the film were going to be there, and I wanted to meet them. Thomas was among them, and we started chatting. I told him what I did and then he told me he was an acting coach. So, I invited him to speak at our events.

Our relationship grew from there. I went to see the 40th anniversary of *The Warriors* with him. Thomas made me an "official warrior" after speaking at one of our events, back in our Pennsylvania office. I met him as a fan, and now we're close friends and business partners. He's co-producing the movie we're working on, *Target*. I executive produced his new movie and we're hosting the premiere at a Hollywood event.

Bill Walsh, CEO of PowerTeam International, America's Small Business Expert, Top Success Coach, Top Business Coach, Author

Bill Walsh is a renowned business coach whose impact on small and large companies across the globe is nothing short of extraordinary. With a remarkable track record of consistently increasing revenues and profits, Bill has become a trusted advisor to entrepreneurs seeking to unlock their businesses' full potential. His expertise has transcended borders, as he has served clients in over 30 countries, leaving a trail of success in his wake.

His exceptional achievements have been recognized on a global scale. He has shared his wealth of knowledge and insights as a lecturer at prestigious institutions like Harvard and the United Nations, captivating audiences with his innovative strategies and practical wisdom. As a testament to his profound impact, Bill is also the best-selling author of the critically acclaimed book, *The Obvious*, which serves as a guiding light for aspiring entrepreneurs. His remarkable abilities have earned him the honor of being ranked among the top 30 business coaches in the world by Guru Magazine, solidifying his position as an industry leader who has transformed the lives of countless individuals and businesses alike. To access Bill's transformative coaching and tap into his wealth of resources, visit www.billwalsh360.com and embark on a journey towards unparalleled growth and success.

Bill and I were first introduced through a mutual friend, CeCe Winans, who was attending one of our events in Las Vegas almost a year ago. CeCe introduced me to Bill, and we hit it off immediately. We have since become good friends and have put together a joint venture, a marketing partnership, to help market our programs to our existing databases.

Scott Patrick Erwin, Actor, Model, Writer

Scott got his start with us during the COVID period and has been with us for about two years. He has taken part in our training and connected with other industry professionals to further his career as an actor, singer, and writer. He is working with us towards making his dreams into a profession.

Michael Stonewall Beaudry, Casting Director

Michael is a casting director who works with independent clients, production companies, directors, ad agencies, musicians, artists, filmmakers, and photographers to provide talent for their projects. Whatever the project, people will go to him to find the right people for the job.

We met when he was invited to one of our events by a mutual friend, a then-photographer, now-director, who was also taking part in the event. We were looking for a casting director and she suggested Michael. Since then, he has come back time and time again to join us for events, helping our talent gain the tools, skills, and confidence they need to find success in this industry.

Fuji Ruiz, Senior Agent, One Model Management

Ryan Colby originally introduced us to Fuji. We've been friends for around 15 years now and I tease him all the time. He was one of the very first major agents who spoke at our event. At the time, he was the head of the women's division of Wilhelmina, which was one of the top three modeling agencies in the world, so he was a major, major agent.

Deneen White, Chief Inspiration Officer, VIP Ignite; President of Talent Services, Talent Management

In business, I am always scouting for good people; it doesn't matter where they come from. When I met Deneen, she was working in the dental industry. I knew her for about three or four years before I texted her, asking if she wanted to become an advocate for us. She never wanted to leave the dental industry, but she had an outstanding personality and I wanted her to get involved.

She didn't know anything about interviewing or podcasts, but after a little persuading—all she had to do was interview talent during an hour-long podcast, once or twice a week—she took me up on the offer. She hit a home run right out the gate. What was supposed to be a single podcast turned into 150 podcasts.

She came on board full-time and now she's President of Talent Services, overseeing all our bookings. Next to me, Alycia and Ryan, she is one of the most knowledgeable people in the industry on modeling, acting, and music. Deneen can run circles around some of our top speakers and is a true asset to the team.

Alycia Kaback, Broadway and TV Producer, Co-founder of VIP Ignite

Alycia was one of the staff I had trained back when I was working as a franchisor. The company she worked for knew it wouldn't be long before they went bankrupt. They said they were closing the corporate office due to cutbacks, calling it a "transition period." We took on a couple of their employees to work in our offices. Alycia and another girl showed up. About a week later, after they had already alleviated the responsibility of a lot of their staff, they bankrupted the company.

The problem was that I had to deliver the news. The girls were all set to move from Florida to New Jersey for their new beginning. It was a job they loved, and I had to tell them that the company they worked for was closing and may have to let them go. It was tough, but we kept in touch.

About a year or so later, when I came up with the idea for

the events, I wanted someone who understood the business at my side. A lot of my original staff had moved on after the office closed. I kept calling, going down my list, and eventually reached Alycia's name. I gave her a call, told her my idea, and asked her if she was interested. The next thing I knew, she was in Philadelphia helping me start VIP Ignite.

We're still together and still going—stronger than ever.

Charles Bodner, BRS/Gage Talent Agent

I met Charles through Billy Magnussen. We were working on Broadway with Pat Addiss while Billy was starring in *Vanya and Sonia and Masha and Spike*. Charles was Billy's manager at the time. We developed a relationship through that and really connected the dots as a result.

Tone Capone, A&R and Development, Vice President of Motown Records, Music Industry

Tone once helped Britney Spears and Akon and was also responsible for helping Pitbull in his early career. Tone was very instrumental in helping us launch the company. We have crossed paths so many times that it has shown me how small this industry is.

Pat Addiss, our Fairy Godmother, Jiminy Cricket, and Mary Poppins all in one, Broadway Producer and Broadway Expert

Pat is an incredible, powerful woman on Broadway. She's stern and will always tell it how it is. She has taught us everything that we needed to know about Broadway and introduced us to some of the biggest stars. For twenty years now, she has been a deep, dear friend and mentor who helped guide us to win multiple Tonys. We wouldn't be where we are without her. She is a true, true friend.

Vincent Rodriguez III, Actor, Voice-Actor, Broadway Actor, Singer, Dancer, Teacher, Mentor

Whenever he is not working on something else, whether on stage or screen, Vincent comes to our events to teach our Inner Circle. He imparts his knowledge, helping new talent understand themselves, hone their craft, and ready themselves to become a part of this industry.

Jeffrey Gurian, Actor, Comedian, Writer, Producer

Originally, Jeffrey was a dentist.

When we first met at Randy Jones' birthday party, he had this crazy hairstyle. I had no idea who he was, but we wound up becoming friends. At the time, we had a radio show on CBS Radio and Howard Stern's Old Studios. I had invited the legendary Joe Franklin to be our very first guest, as well as Jeffrey. Unbeknownst to me, the two of them knew each other. The moment Joe walked into the room, he remembered Jeffrey as a dentist, not as a comedian and writer. That was one of the funniest encounters I've ever had.

Jeffrey is an absolute darling and a staple in the comedy community. He works with everyone from Ben Stiller and Jerry Seinfeld to Eddie Murphy and Chris Rock. And for us, he just came out to our event for our movie premiere. It was awesome.

Roxanne Messina Captor, Director, Producer, Writer

Roxanne is the protégé of Francis Ford Coppola and has a resume beyond belief at the highest possible level.

We met at a dinner party in Malibu. The party, hosted by the then head of AI development for Google, had some incredible people in attendance. I ended up being seated with the host, along with a woman who was the heir to the Pillsbury Company (she had just sold a house to Taylor Swift for $25 million the day before the party), another woman whose husband was the founder of the Grammys, Pat Addiss, and of course, Roxanne.

I started talking to Roxanne and explained what we did, which she thought was the most amazing thing. A few months later, she flew out to Pennsylvania and spoke at our office. Since then, she's spoken at many of our events. The other guests from that party are still close friends of mine as well.

Robert Russell, VP of Warner Brothers Casting *(retired)*

I met Robert at our second event. We were making calls to get some agents to come to the event, and we were struggling to get anybody because we were brand new. Eventually, we got in contact with a woman who ran a small agency in Philadelphia. She gave us a list of her contacts and on that list was Robert Russell.

He had recently retired from his position as Vice President of Casting for Warner Brothers. Of course, I wanted him at the event. He was what I wanted VIP Ignite to represent. We wanted the best people in the world. We wanted this guy.

She wasn't even sure if she could get him to agree, but she called him anyway. Robert called back saying he'd do the event. It was crazy.

The day of the event came, and we were all nervously waiting for him to show up. We didn't know what to expect; maybe some kind of Hollywood entourage or someone dressed to the T in his suit and tie. When he came through the door, he looked like a bald John Lennon.

He had little, round Lennon glasses, was super skinny, wearing a Google t-shirt and ripped jeans with both arms covered in a full sleeve of tattoos. He was the nicest guy in the world, and I remember thinking, *So this is casting? This is cool, I can dig it. I'm wearing a full suit and he's wearing a t-shirt, cool.* Now 20 years later, I've risen to his level and am wearing t-shirts every day.

Patrick Quagliano, Head of Stella Adler, Acting Coach of the Stars

Patrick has trained everyone from Johnny Depp to Meryl Streep to Al Pacino to Chris Pine. He's worked with some of the biggest names; he's the one who trained them. Patrick is also the on-site acting coach for JJ Abrams and Ron Howard Productions.

Marthe Reynolds, VP Island Def Jam *(retired)*

When I first got to speak with her, Marthe was a female executive. She was the VP of P. Diddy's record label, once had Jay-Z sleeping on her couch, and now raises championship horses in the Midwest. She is a legend, like the Quincy Jones of the hip-hop world.

Robert Galinsky, Head of Robert Galinsky Coaching, TED and TEDX Talk Speaker

Robert has worked with some big names in the industry and coaches many of our clients and students. He attends many of our events and hosts workshops that help them express more, to be more open and confident in themselves, and to improvise a little bit—to take what they're given and turn it into something better.

Ryan Colby, Head of Ryan Colby Management

Ryan manages a wide collection of models and actors, helping them to look and feel fierce. When he comes to work with us at VIP Ignite, he directs many of our shoots, making sure that we have stellar photographers, hair and makeup, and wardrobe. He's the guy that keeps the train moving.

Jesse Heiman, Actor, The World's Greatest Extra

He's super quirky, weird, and gentle—like a big teddy bear.

We met him through a Los Angeles-based agency when one of their agents, who represented Jesse, was coming out to speak at one of our events. She got us in contact with him because we had a lot of new talent. One of the first genres they work in is doing background work, being in the scene and on set. He's the man who made a ten-plus year career out of that, being in multiple Academy Award-winning movies.

He made a documentary about his life in the industry. It's interesting because so many people come into this industry wanting to be the star, wanting to be the lead. But they don't realize that being an extra is how you get your waivers. Jesse is incredible because he has made a career doing just that, and at the highest possible level.

Phil Sullivan, Model, America's Next Top Model Contestant

Before we met him, Phil was discovered by Ryan Colby. Ryan was developing Phil and getting him placed with some huge brands. But Phil decided he wanted to submit himself for *America's Next Top Model*.

Now, if you're not familiar with the show, understand that back then, they didn't want people who were already being represented. If you were represented, you had to break your contract and sign an agreement saying you had never been signed. It created this storyline that you were just a normal person. Phil went ahead, broke his contract with Ryan, and Ryan blew his top. He didn't speak to Phil for over a decade. He was done with Phil.

Fast forward a bit and Fuji Ruiz, who was working on the show, invited Phil to come to one of our events. We had never met the guy before, but Ryan was furious, even saying he wouldn't come to the event if Phil planned to attend.

Anyway, cutting a long story short, Phil and Ryan ended up making amends and becoming friends. Now Phil has spoken at dozens of our events. He inspires our new talent to go out and do what he's doing, no matter who they are. He inspired kids like James Johnson, who, when we met him, was the geekiest kid you'd ever meet: no clothes, no style, a complete train wreck. But he wanted to be like Phil, so Ryan signed him. A year later, the two of them, Phil and James, were walking side by side for the New York Fashion Week.

LETTER FROM THE AUTHOR

I live my life working with actors, models, and musicians. I spend my time working with casting directors, agents, and producers. I've invested hundreds of thousands of dollars on Broadway and seen this industry from many perspectives. I went from one thing to another, climbing higher and higher, and now I'm somewhere that most people only dream of.

Over the years, I've heard stories of people being taken advantage of financially, emotionally, and physically. Behind closed doors, the industry isn't all glitz and glamour. Hearing those stories has only deepened my passion for working in this industry and helping to aid the people who want to be a part of it.

I believe it's my moral obligation to help connect you with people who are honest, supportive, and direct. You deserve to be supported and protected so that you can succeed in a world that is often perceived as being just as toxic as it is confusing.

I never thought I'd pursue a career in the world of entertainment. Even though I didn't initially chase a career in the industry, I've always had an interest in it and a passion for it. Since participating in school plays from high school through college, to writing manuscripts; the creativity and dedication of those who could make their way in the entertainment industry fascinated me.

I would spend hours searching for clues and cracks in the proverbial door that would allow me the opportunity to become *somebody* within the industry. I invested in classes and training only to find that the entertainment business is challenging.

I faced that feeling of disappointment and felt the sting of rejection before I even started. It was a motivator to try even harder and push even further. But it was difficult.

I put things on hold, opened a restaurant, and found success in the hospitality industry. Then my opportunity appeared. I wanted a change, got my foot in the door, and then blew it off its hinges. However, in the beginning, I didn't have a mentor or any real guidance. I had to learn the ins and outs by myself, but I did it. I learned everything I could and spoke to everyone I could. I made connections, good and bad. Once I started down this road, nothing stopped me.

Without having someone there to guide you and give you the best start possible, it feels like you're making every step in the dark. It's that feeling of upset and uncertainty that was the driving force to creating VIP Ignite and Truth Management.

So, for people who are struggling in this industry, for those who have suffered because of it, and for those who have come *so* close to their dreams only to have them dashed because of outside influence, I want to set you on the right path by giving you the recipe for success.

Sometimes, *who* you know can be even more valuable than what you know. So, start making real connections and taking real steps toward your success in this industry right now.

Michael Fomkin
The Connection King, VIP Ignite / Truth Management

CONTENTS

— Interviews from the Industry, Part Seven
   - Michael Stonewall Beaudry
   - Alexandria De Rossi
   - Phil Sullivan
   - Santino Fontana
   - Jesse Heiman
   - Scott Patrick Erwin
   - Thomas G. Waites
   - Les Brown

INTRODUCTION

IMAGINE that tomorrow you could . . .

- be face-to-face with an Academy Award-winning director, talking about your ambitions and hearing their advice;

- speak directly to a casting director who works with some of the biggest names in Hollywood, and get tips on auditioning right from the source;

- play your demo for the producer of a major record label and get their immediate feedback;

- meet the casting agent for a major make-up or clothing line and they could tell you exactly what type of modeling would best suit you.

Imagine tomorrow was the perfect opportunity for you and your career. Would you take it? Would you be ready for it?

To make it in the entertainment business, whether that be in the film, music, or modeling industry, you need to have the drive, as well as the talent. Few people have the talent, but even fewer have the drive, that fire-in-the-gut yearning to succeed no matter what it takes. But let's say you have that drive. You've put all you can into your craft and worked hard to shape yourself into the best you can be. What's next?

For new and aspiring talent, you might feel like you're jumping through every hoop, hoping to get that first job. Sometimes it can feel like the only way into the industry is to be born into it or to be discovered in a chance encounter. That is a discouraging and disempowering mindset to have, thinking that you can only succeed in this industry if you're favored by fate.

It's a mindset that often stops many people from even trying to take that first step and get their foot in the door, let alone trying to find a way to keep it open. But, of course, there is something that these two scenarios have in common, something that we often forget. That is that both are completely out of your control.

So, the question is, what can you control?

VIP Ignite was founded to give you control over your career, to be the bridge to the dream of starring on Broadway, acting in Hollywood, and walking the runway in Paris. It was founded to give new talent the chance, not just to network, but to create real relationships and build the kind of foundation that can start their career. We are here to help you take that next step.

People who are struggling in the industry likely don't know how to make the right choices, let alone the right connections that will help them become successful. The people who had the dream and the determination, but somehow didn't see it come to fruition, are missing something. They didn't have the right people to help them find out what those things are. I was the same when I first transitioned into this industry.

When I began, I knew nothing about what I was doing, with only a handful of connections to help me get started. People would tell me they knew what they were doing, whether they did or not. I had to trust them. Thankfully for me, they didn't have any motives other than wanting to give something back. They were the kind of people that had a wider passion and saw the bigger picture. They had an idea but didn't know how to accomplish it and decided to lend me a hand because I knew how to do it. I just didn't have the right information to start.

Whenever you make that jump to something new, no matter what it might be, there are obstacles. There are all of those new faces and new voices that end up leading you down the wrong path. But there are always a few that will steer you in the *right* direction; *you just have to know how to find them.*

Despite all the difficulties, you also have to remember that sometimes you have to fall and fail in order to appreciate what you have achieved when you get to the other side. It's always easier when you have a hand to help you up and push you onward.

There's a lot of misinformation out there, especially about this industry. The internet is readily accessible, but difficult to navigate. Knowing how and where to search for the right information is crucial. For instance, Google is a trashcan of information about the entertainment industry.

You can find anything you want about the industry by googling top models, chart-topping musicians, and big stars. It's a great tool, I'll admit. But there's no clear guide to show what these people did to get where they are. Think about it. You can research, subscribe to, and follow celebrities on the likes of Google, Instagram, Twitter, TikTok, and YouTube. You see them live their lives, read their stories, watch their videos, and follow their journeys. Maybe you get an idea of how they achieved their success, but there isn't an easy way to figure out how to replicate that success for yourself. Google doesn't publish a step-by-step guide on how to become successful, because there is no answer or published path.

Most celebrities will give a few bits of advice here and there and become an inspiration to their fans. They don't have the time to go out and teach people the tips and tricks of how they succeeded in the industry.

Even if you somehow find the right information through

a quick Google search, when it comes to resources, where do you start? A lot of big companies have the budgets, hundreds of thousands of dollars a year, to bring in advisors and professionals to come up with new ideas, to work with their staff, and to motivate their teams.

You want to use the same expert resources, but you don't know who they are, how to reach them, or even whether you can afford the costs of hiring them. Honestly, there is a good chance that you don't even know these people exist as a resource.

In the entertainment industry, for example, there's no easy way to find who the casting director is for a Disney film coming out in six months, unless you already know that person or are already in the company. Another example would be the cosmetics industry. It's hard to find a high-end photographer without knowing their agent first. Unless you've already got your foot in the door with certain people and companies, it's near impossible to take advantage of the same resources available to people who are already through the door.

But that's not how it should be.

People, stepping into the industry, see this mess of information, and do not know what is right or even valuable. I asked myself, and those who had helped me, "Why don't we create something to help people that were like me? What if there was something that could help guide those people who are looking to make the leap and become a part of this industry?"

It's always exciting to be in a world where you get to add something, create something new, and share something that never existed. It's kind of like a train set or modeling kit where the foundation and tools are provided, but the creativity is in your hands. Now, with VIP Ignite, we have created a safe space for fresh faces and new talent to pursue their dreams with all the right tools close to hand.

The thing is, when you go onto the internet you can find all these people who have gotten close to the sun, but never got to touch it. The kind of actors who never truly made it and became acting coaches, or the musicians who never had their big break and became teachers. They're making their income from that and that's good; they still get to do something they love. But I don't think it's fair. If you want to become a teacher, then make that happen and teach a new generation of talent. If you're going to be a casting director, strive to become a casting director. When your goal is to be an actor, do everything in your power to become an actor.

Don't sell yourself short, no matter what it is you want to do.

You can advise others who might be starting out once you've achieved your goals, but you'll never really know the ins and outs of every aspect of the industry if you've only focused on your corner. You can advise on being an actor, on playing music, on walking the runway, or even on what to do when you walk through the doors of an audition. But you'll only be able to give your thoughts on that one part of the industry. There's no way an actor could give truly valuable advice on the thought processes of an agent or casting director, for example. They might think they can, but in reality, they can't. They don't know enough about that job—that world— to advise anyone on how to interact effectively within it.

Many people get taken advantage of in this industry. They do not have the right information, connections, and avenues. I want to make sure this does not happen to the clients and talent who choose to work with VIP Ignite. We coach our talent so that they develop the skills and confidence that they need to be successful in the entertainment industry. We introduce them to the right people and give them real connections that will help them achieve their goals and become truly successful.

For us, connections are a resource. They are one of the most valuable resources you can have at your disposal. It's like having a skeleton key. When you've made those connections, it opens the door to unlimited possibilities.

Without those connections, you're locked out. You're alone. You're trying to look at a map with no directions, absolutely none. But when you start to see little dots appear on the map, you can start on the path to your destiny. Each of those dots is a new and valuable connection to someone in the industry. They're not simply points; they're living, breathing human beings with the knowledge and experience to guide you in the right direction and down the right path.

I've seen so many different maps from so many different people, though the most successful journeys are from those who have made real connections. Those connections could be good or bad with a few mistakes here and there, but the reason they are successful is because they are connected. Without connections, you're stuck. You don't move at all and you're just going to stay in the same place.

So, you're on this journey, somewhere along the road, whether at the start or stuck at a crossroads. You've gone from point to point, but now you can't go any further. Each little distance you've traveled, you've become that little bit more knowledgeable. You've become that little bit stronger. You've gotten that little bit better at what you're doing. Still, you're struggling to get to your destination. Even if they're just starting out, most people will have done the basics; tried to hone their craft and done a little bit of research. Yet everything comes to a standstill at some point because they don't know what to do next.

This book is the start of something new and an insider's guide to understanding the entertainment industry and building the strategies you need to keep connections in it. I'm going to share my journey through this industry with you, my highs and lows, and my ultimate success in creating VIP Ignite. I'm going to give you all the ins and outs and the things I wish I had known back when I first started.

You might not know where your destination is, only that you want to succeed. But now this road you're on is about to take a different turn. You're going to take those next steps. And in the end, you'll wind up some place even better than you could have imagined.

CHAPTER 1

TAKING THAT LEAP

There was a time when I was somewhere different. A time when I decided to change my direction. Once, twice, and then again for good measure. I was once working at the front desk in retail, and then the guy making pizzas in his own restaurant. But now, somehow, I'm sitting with celebrities and the greats of the entertainment industry. Now, I get to go to Costa Rica and meet the likes of Tony Robbins and do all these things I never thought I could do.

I get to do all these things that most people reserve only for their dreams. I never would have done any of these things had it not been for the people I met and the things I learned from them. Good or bad, the connections I have made are everything. They've guided me through an industry I knew nothing about, and my whole life has changed because of them.

GETTING TO THE GLITZ AND GLAMOUR

Originally, I didn't set out to work in the entertainment industry.

Believe it or not, I used to work in sales at Patek Philippe, a high-end watch retailer, in Manhattan. I kind of ended up there after college. The company was expanding, and when working the floor, I started to take an interest in the marketing and advertising aspects of the business. This included online retail, which was still a relatively new development for reaching consumers. Every step into this new world fascinated me, and I quickly became one of the company's youngest managers, all because I wanted to be a part of the growth.

During my time with the company, I had the privilege of rubbing shoulders with many successful people. The kind of people who could easily afford to spend $20,000, $50,000, or even $500,000 on a watch. Even though I was only 21 years old, I was building a rapport with all these big shots, the people who were where I wished I could be, just so I could sell them a watch with a few accessories on the side.

I found myself getting all sorts of passing advice from stockbrokers, attorneys, doctors, and even the odd celebrity. At that point, I realized I had an itch that I couldn't scratch. It was a bug that was constantly telling me that there was no potential for growth from my current position. I might climb a little higher, but ultimately, I would still sell watches on Madison Avenue. That would be my plateau.

I wasn't sure what I wanted to do, but I knew I didn't want to plateau. I wanted to be doing something that felt new and exciting. In college, I used to deliver pizzas. So I thought, why not open a small business and grow it as far as I could?

I left retail and turned my sights to hospitality. I borrowed some money from my family and opened an Italian restaurant called Mr. Nino's, in Northern New Jersey. It was in an area where there were nine other Italian restaurants and small mom-and- pop pizzerias. Looking back, maybe it wasn't the smartest move, but I saw it as an opportunity to put the things I had learned to use.

At the watch retailer, we had a marketing campaign where clients could exchange old watches for any of the new watches we sold. So, I did the same thing—turn in your old Italian restaurant menu for a new one. Customers could order a onetime special from us for $5, and when we delivered it, the deal was they would give us their old Italian delivery menu. The deal was an exchange of their old restaurant menu for our new one. By doing this, the hope was the next time they ordered food, our menu would be at the top of the stack. I used every guerrilla marketing technique that I could think of.

I even hired kids from the local school to dress up as pizza slices and direct people to Mr. Nino's, instead of the other restaurants on the street. By the time we closed our doors, we were one of two out of the original nine restaurants left. Guess I must have done something right.

But before I decided to close those doors, I'd felt the same as when I had worked in retail. I loved what I did, but I was plateauing again. If you've never worked in the restaurant industry, it's a lot of work. It's seven days a week for twelve hours a day. It's coming home covered in flour and smelling of garlic. It's chaotic and I loved it. However, despite enjoying it, I was burning myself out. I wanted something new, and I wanted something more. I'll admit that, after I closed the doors and sold the restaurant, I didn't really know what to do with myself. I didn't know what path to take next, so I went online.

I started searching for business opportunities. I began looking into franchising and eventually I came across this ad.

Would you like to own your own modeling agency?
Be a judge at beauty contests?
Meet local celebrities?

I had spent the last five years working twelve hours a day in the restaurant industry and there I was reading an advert for a job where I'd get to judge beauty contests and hang out with all these incredible people.

It was something different; it was something new, and it sounded like the ideal job. As you'd expect, I applied right away. What you might not expect is that I got a call from an office in Orlando the next day. They asked if I wanted a chance at franchising, with one catch—I had to be at their office in two days. I got myself a plane ticket that day, along with a copy of *GQ*. Since I had spent the past half-decade in a restaurant, I didn't know what to bring or what to wear to a modeling agency. I just packed the smartest thing I could find and went to board the plane with the magazine in hand.

In Orlando, I found a buzzing office, overflowing with employees. People were packed three to an office, and unlike me, they were dressed to a T. It was like nothing I had ever seen before, but there was this incredible energy.

During the franchisers' orientation, I learned that eModels, the parent company, wanted to revolutionize the way modeling worked. They weren't really a modeling company, that was just their hook to get you through the door. They were more like a software company, and their software was designed to redesign how agencies were doing business.

The intention was to create a database that could be broken down not only by hair color, eye color, or height; but also by statistics like dress size, cup size, waist size. The software could even categorize by more niche features, like if the model had tattoos or whether they could speak French, for example.

You could use this software to find models of every shape, size, ethnicity, and gender, and search for any combination of traits that you needed for a project. In just a few minutes, you could see hundreds of models that matched your requirements alongside their availability. It was going to be a database that would allow models to take control of their careers by registering, paying a fee, uploading their portfolios, and submitting themselves to castings listed on the site.

Now, this was back in 2001, the average modeling company didn't even have computers, let alone access to something like this. It was revolutionary. They were literally five years ahead of the curve and they knew it. The franchise buy-in price was $10,000. It was a gamble. I remember asking if I could think it over and they gave me twenty-four hours to *come to a decision.*

The next thing I remember is starting my two-week crash course on the modeling industry with my bank account feeling considerably lighter. Between sessions, I walked around the offices asking everyone what they did and how. From sales to software, I wanted to know everything. I watched everything they did and memorized everything I could, even down to the color of the walls and the models of the chairs. By the time they were finished with me, I was finished with them. I knew enough about the business to know what worked and what didn't. I could figure out the reasons doing something one way was better than another. I went home ready and prepared to start hiring staff and talent scouts.

The talent scouts would be the backbone of the company, going from place to place looking for talent and inviting potential models to come to our offices for an audition. We set the first scout orientation for 9 am, September 11, 2001. I remember when the first tower of the World Trade Center was hit. Our office was about two hours away, in Princeton, New Jersey. And I remember the panic as people rushed to check their phones. It was crazy.

After 9/11, no one wanted to work in New York City and most people wanted to relocate or find something new entirely. So, when we scheduled our next orientation, we had almost 90 people come in dressed to the T in their suits and ties, waving around these 5-star resumes. The people I hired that day stayed with me longer than anyone else. I don't know if the camaraderie fostered around that tragic time played a part, but they were the most amazing group of scouts I have ever hired.

Within two months we outgrew the shared suite and were forced to find a new space. We had nearly a hundred people a night who wanted to be models and actors. I started each day at 8 am and worked with the scouts and talent until 10 pm. But my day didn't stop there. When everyone else went home, I uploaded all the pictures from the day into the database. I'd get home around 4 am and crash on the couch, only to start it all over again four hours later. I had gone from working twelve to sixteen-hour days in the restaurant to working twenty-hour days at the agency, and I loved it. I wanted more.

Now, not all the franchises that had been set up were successful. Some owners wanted to do things their own way, but really, from what I learned in Orlando, there was a system that worked; they just weren't following it. So, I began buying franchises that were failing, purchasing their equipment, sending in my scouts, and following the system. Soon I owned ten franchises and could turn the business profitable within thirty days of receiving the keys. It was a challenge for sure, but I had the drive. I had the passion for it, and I was having fun.

I would hire additional scouts, train them the same way I did all the others, and get them out scouting quality talent within the first week. At our first open call for each office, we had over fifty people looking to audition. It was great to meet all these amazing new aspiring models and actors, feel the constant buzz, and see the excitement.

In less than two years, the company announced that it had gotten a big investor and was going international. They brought in all the franchise owners for a big meeting where we got to meet the investor. It was Lou Pearlman.

He was a billionaire, the owner of an airline, and a renowned record producer. This was the guy who had discovered the likes of the Backstreet Boys and NSYNC. Now he was looking to invest and become a part of the company. He wanted to bring music to the table, expanding our reach. The idea was to help budding musicians along with aspiring models and actors while scouting potential stars through the database. Musicians could come into the office to audition, have their records uploaded, and then have Lou Pearlman listen to them.

It was an incredible opportunity, and he was an incredible guy. He was heavyset, very friendly, and very personable. He invited us to parties and introduced us to all these celebrities in his circles. I just remember looking around and thinking, *I can't believe this. I used to work in retail and own a little restaurant. Now I'm drinking with Hulk Hogan and the Backstreet Boys.* It was like the next part of the dream was coming true.

So, Lou came onboard, and the company change the financial to this kind of revenue share where they would charge the agencies by billing the franchises instead of the offices. Looking back, this was a horrible idea, but I was still new to all of this, and it didn't really have any immediate effect on my life. I was responsible for ten franchises and around five hundred employees. They were my priority. As long as it didn't affect how my businesses operated and how my team functioned, I had no complaints.

Soon, however, things began to go awry.

The checks started coming up short. I had to pay out-of-pocket to cover expenses because the company wasn't sending us what was owed. It wasn't small amounts either. $500 here or there wouldn't have been great, but instead of that, they were owing us closer to $500,000 each time. I was sitting with ten major offices. It mounted up quickly to top it all off, when Lou came onboard, we all developed an issue with the Attorney General. We didn't know it then, but the Attorney General had a much bigger fish that they were looking for.

They started phoning up the offices, but Lou had a better way of working with them. You could never meet a more charismatic guy; he worked his charm and shooed them away for a while. He came back and told us they were targeting agencies for price fixing, one of which was a small company called Wilhelmina. After some negotiating, Wilhelmina accepted the deal, making us the owners of the Wilhelmina models. And since it was all broken down into shares, I ended up with one third of the company.

It was pretty exciting, but we still had the underlying issue of Lou. He wasn't sending the checks out, despite the fact we now had Wilhelmina also invested. There was a lot of cash and excuses being passed around and soon the Attorney General came back onto the scene. They started playing a different game. They called up and asked about Lou in specific.

I found out that this transcontinental airline he owned was a "paper" company. From the accounting firm and PR for the company, all of it was owned by Lou and all faked to make everything look legit. It was one of the largest Ponzi schemes ever concocted and when the opportunity came for him to be a part of our company, it was his chance to make money again. As soon as he signed on, unknown to all of us, his claws started siphoning money from our company to investors in that scheme he had created.

After the phone call, I remember just being blown away. I had no words and when we confronted Lou, neither did he. He tried to show us all these numbers and pictures, but when that didn't convince us it was all legit, he shut down and stopped talking. The next thing we knew, the checks weren't being cut in half; they were being cut by 90%. This guy was going to bankrupt us.

That was when things started to blow up. The only thing we could do was try to sue him, but then he decided that he was going to sue us for $100 million. I was sitting in the office when they told me I was being sued for $100 million by Lou Pearlman. The only thing I could think was that this was just another façade; just a bluff to trick us into backing down. Well, the next thing I knew, we were hiring an attorney to defend us because none of us were willing to back down.

I flew down to Orlando, and they brought Lou in.

Just a little over two years earlier, I had thought this guy was awesome. But when I sat in that courtroom, I got to see his true colors. Through a charismatic guise, he had mastered the art of puppeteering people's feelings to the point where you wouldn't think to look behind the curtain to see the train wreck that was going on. He was lying through his teeth, saying he never knew any of us and that I was only vaguely familiar despite attending numerous events and parties at his side. I remember being in complete shock. Our attorney told me that he could say whatever he wants, truth or not. Still, I wanted to believe that there was no way that he could get away with such blatant lies.

To make a long story short, without detailing the entire proceedings, our attorney pulled out all these records, accounts, and communications of everything that had been happening. It was our proof against his word. Then, after about six months, Lou suddenly decided that he wanted to drop the lawsuit. He said he would pay us $150,000 to go away. I'll be honest, we kind of did. I convinced my partners that it would be better to cut our losses and start anew. Take what we have and make it into something better.

Lou wrote us the check. And not even two days later, his business partner committed suicide; Lou went on the run. It was all over the news. I tried to stay calm, see it as a blessing because everything was finally catching up with him. But then I got a call.

Despite everything we had gone through, we had to declare bankruptcy. The company was gone. Only a month before, I was hanging out with the Backstreet Boys and now I didn't even know what to say. Even when the authorities caught up with Lou, all the money was gone. When getting the money back through the liquidation of Lou's assets, the original investors came first We weren't even a consideration. Everything— the company, the money, and the partnership— was gone.

It was a mess, but I still had my employees to think about. They were *my* responsibility–my scouts, my models, my staff. I couldn't just leave them with nothing. For the next 30 days, one of my partners and I covered the wages of our staff and the additional expenses. Together, we rebuilt our database from scratch. We relaunched the company under a new brand, but I wound up selling my partnership to him. For the second time in my life, I was asking myself, what do I do with my life now?

STARTING SOMETHING NEW, AGAIN

I came to another junction in my life, but this time, the people I knew weren't enough to create a new path for me to take. At least, not in the beginning. I had friends all over the country. All these offices, and people I knew through my staff, talent, and scouts, didn't have any real connections in the industry, per se. The only connection in the industry was Lou, and he was in jail. It wasn't the best connection to have. But then I remembered one thing from my years working as a franchisor, an idea that was thrown around that could be the start of something new.

The idea was to host an event where models and talent from all over the country could come to be introduced to the industry's specialists—agents and scouts that could give new talent a chance. It would be an event where we'd reach out to agencies around the world, pay them to attend, and even pay for their hotels and flights. The talent would come to them. We'd have concerts, talks, and meet and greets. We'd bring an array of new models and actors to the agencies rather than the agencies having to do the legwork.

Now, this was the dream, the end goal. But first I needed to find a way to kick-start it. No one else was trying to do anything like this, and I wanted to learn the industry. I really wanted to understand it. I was so fascinated by it that this idea just seemed like a good leap.

I made a new path and decided I'd start small, only 100 people or so. But when I called several agencies in New York, they turned me down. They wanted photos and portfolios.

They wanted people with experience. They didn't want to take time out of their schedule to come and see a bunch of newbies. It was a bump in the road. So, I tried a different tactic. I went to Craigslist and wrote an ad. It was only a few sentences. I wrote it exactly how I spoke and at the end, I added, *oh, and by the way, lunch will be provided.* I posted it and sat there thinking, what's the worst that could happen?

By the next morning, I had gotten about 400 responses to that ad. I had writers, journalists, casting directors, actors, producers, musicians, a ring announcer from the WWE, a reality TV star who had his own show on the History Channel, and even one of the producers who worked on Michael Jackson's album, *Thriller.*

My mind had been so focused on finding agents, it had never even dawned on me that there were so many more people in this industry and they all might want to be a part of the event. Suddenly it went from an event for new talent to a 360-degree view of the industry where anyone who wanted to discover something new could come and find it. I saw what this could become if this first event turned out to be a success.

I picked twelve people out of the 400 that responded, and you know something? I never had to reach out to anybody ever again. The first event was a success and after that, the dream spiralled.

Those twelve people started to introduce us to other people and the people they introduced us to, introduced us to more people, and then all of those great people were reaching out to me to come to our events. The little road I had started on, had become a highway. It was magical but I guess you could say destiny had a hand in it, too.

The day before I had put the ad up, the writer's strike in New York had happened. Because of that, many writers, producers, and actors were out of work. So, when I posted my ad, it just happened to be at the top. It was the first thing a lot of them saw and for them it was just a chance to speak at an event, do a gig, and ultimately get paid. It was their darkest moment that became our brightest light, and it was at my darkest moment that they became my brightest light. Everyone at the first event took a chance and after that, the dream just took off.

VIP Ignite was officially launched in 2006 and we were able to launch Truth Management in 2020. Every connection we have made over the years has been a catalyst for growth. It allowed us to reach higher and higher levels of success and help more and more aspiring talent to take the right steps toward their own success stories.

CHAPTER 2

CONNECTIONS ARE KEY

**I always tell people that your net worth
equals your network.
You've got to get out there,
 meet people and shake hands.
Be seen, let people see you, and eventually,
you'll connect with the right people
in the right place at the right time.**
– Tone Capone

Connections are like a resource. They open doors, let you explore unlimited possibilities, and take you down new roads that let you go to places you'd never imagined. You need to have connections. They give you the dots to mark your map and a collection of new travel locations. Without them, you're navigating the industry with no direction.

I am reminded of a time way back in 2003, when my old agency did an open casting call in New York. I was working with a woman in PR who was also freelancing as a music writer. She was good at her work and was keen on exposing others to the ins and outs of the industry. One day, she asked me if I would like an artist she was working with to talk to our talent, to give them an insight into a different world. His name was Pitbull, and she did her best to reassure me that it would be beneficial for my models. I didn't think it was a big deal, and I certainly didn't see any harm in it.

At that time, Pitbull was still a year away from releasing his debut album, *M.I.A.M.I.*, but he came to speak to a collection of new talent about the music industry.

I was gripped by every word he said, but one girl stood up, clicked her heels, and started walking out. We never wanted people walking out during presentations because not only was it rude, but it encouraged others to think, *well if she's leaving, should I go too?* It was kind of a herd mentality back then. If one model walked, they all walked.

So, I got up and talked to her. I asked her why she was leaving, and her response was one that still stands out to me to this day. She said that she was there for the modeling, that she didn't know who the music guy was, and she didn't care to learn. She stormed off thinking that we were wasting her time. I still wonder if she regrets her decision.

If she had stayed, she would have possibly had Pitbull as a connection. She could have starred in music videos or promotional material. But no, she didn't see the value of that connection and walked out.

That attitude is still something that infuriates me. People have this idea that each part of the entertainment industry is separate, and that's just not true. Here was a man who took time out of his day to share some knowledge with you, and you should appreciate that. If someone who has experience offers you advice, even if you don't think it's relevant to you, listen to them. These are busy people who have taken time out to help you and to give you knowledge and perspectives that you didn't have before.

There is opportunity in every connection you make, no

matter what part of the industry they work in. You never know when something will be useful and the more you know, the better off you'll be in the future. So, when we are putting on our events, we don't care if you come just for the acting, the modeling, or the music. You should come to our events ready to meet everyone from every corner of the industry.

Imagine it: you sign up with an agency and go to an audition. You are one of the last contenders for the role, and the casting director asks you, "Tell me something about yourself." Now, you had attended one of our events only a week before and had the opportunity to meet Howard McGillin, an amazing actor on stage and screen. In your answer, you mention to the director that you had the opportunity to have an interesting conversation with Howard, and suddenly the director is a lot more interested in you. You didn't give the generic answer about wanting to follow a dream *and* you have a connection, a name in the industry. You are suddenly much more interesting to that director. Something so small has the potential to help you stand out from the crowd and seriously influence your life and your career.

I remember working with Billy Magnussen while he was working on Broadway with Pat Addiss. She had cast him for the role of Spike in *Vanya and Sonia and Masha and Spike*. From that, he was nominated for a Tony Award for Best Featured Actor in a Play. He was a young, up-and-coming Broadway actor who was Tony-nominated, working with the likes of Sigourney Weaver, and it was that connection that got him his big break in the film industry.

Meryl Streep came to the show and afterward reached out to Sigourney Weaver, saying that she was going to be starring in a new Disney movie called *Into the Woods* and that she wanted to submit Billy for a part in the film. He wound up getting the part, playing the role of Rapunzel's Prince, which just kicked off his career. Literally, a year later, he was starring in *Bridge of Spies* directed by Steven Spielberg. He worked with Disney again in *Aladdin* in 2019. Then in 2021, he starred in the most recent James Bond movie, *No Time to Die*. He's done a ton of stuff, and all of that came from that original circle of connections. It came from creating that investment, bringing that show to life. All of it had this rippling effect that changed people's lives.

But . . . you have to remember that names aren't always everything. They give you direct connections, but sometimes your greatest connections can come from taking a chance.

I was walking in Times Square one day with Deric Angelettie, the Grammy-winning musician and producer, when a kid came up to us trying to sell his demo CD for ten dollars. He followed us for a few minutes, telling us about his music, desperate for us to buy his album. We weren't interested, but eventually, I turned to the kid and told him that if he really wanted his music heard, he should just give this man his CD. The kid refused. He gave up trying to sell us his CD, like that young model who lost a chance to connect when she walked out. Had that young man given Deric Angelettie his demo, that connection might have changed his life forever. You don't always know who the important people are, so you have to stay open to every opportunity.

THE RIGHT IMPRESSION CAN CHANGE YOUR DESTINY

So, let's say you take that chance. You have the opportunity to shoot your shot. How do you turn that chance into a real connection?

Well, you make your most valuable connections by giving someone the "right" impression. The reason they will have given you a chance is that, whether it was for your skills or your passion, they saw something in you. The reason they will want to connect with you is usually that they like you in some way. Giving someone the right impression is so important because it can really make or break your career.

We first met Robert Russell when we hosted our second event after becoming VIP Ignite. We had rented a hotel where Robert arrived in the late afternoon. Dinner wasn't to be served for a few hours. Well, he's a diabetic and his blood sugar wound up dropping. He asked the hotel manager for a slice of bread, but they gave him the excuse that, for whatever unknown reason, they couldn't give him anything because the food wasn't ready. So, in traditional fashion, they just said, "We'll see what we can do."

Alycia completely ignored the hotel manager and walked right into the kitchen. She was absolutely having none of it. She went in, demanded food for Robert, telling them he was one of our speakers, and that he needed something to eat now!

They fixed him up a plate of something, which she brought back for Robert.

In that one, a rather comical moment, our destiny was created, and here's how.

When you're somebody at the level that Robert was in his life, you've seen it all. You have been through the highest of highs and the lowest of lows. He was so dedicated to his craft that he gave up parts of himself to come out on the other side. And the one thing he recognized and respected without question was the ability to get things done.

You have to get things done when you're on set. There's nobody babying people. You have to figure it out as you go. You overcome, you adapt, you survive, and you get things done. There are no excuses.

Robert was so impressed with what Alycia did for him that he took us and the company under his wing. He opened up his entire black book. He was the one who introduced us to Robert Galinsky, who then introduced us to Pat Addiss, who eventually introduced us to Roxanne Messina Captor. It was the connection that helped us win thirty-eight awards and six Tonys.

Had it not been for that one piece of bread situation and the impression it created, Robert would have come and just left. Honestly, we might not be in business now without it.

I can give another example too, but from another perspective.

When we first started out, we were really into music. I found a band that could have been one of the most incredible bands in the world. I invited them to meet Robert because, when it came to music, he knew his stuff. They had a really great idea and wanted to do a reality show.

The band had been traveling around the country in a

CHAPTER 2 CONNECTIONS ARE KEY

beat-up old van going from show to show, self-funding the whole trip. Each new show was funded by what they made from their previous shows. It was an interesting premise.

They told me about the time when they broke down in the middle of nowhere. They had no gas, and a farmer came along in his old pickup offering his help. But after noticing they were a band, he only helped them in exchange for them playing at his daughter's birthday party. Cut to an hour later, and they were playing in the middle of a cornfield somewhere. There would be other segments as well because they were relatively new in their career, building their fan base through social media. They would randomly pick fans up for the show or drop off tickets in person.

At the time, I thought connecting them with Robert would be a great idea because he had worked so closely with some of the biggest names on TV. I invited the band to dinner with him and told them there was only one rule: Don't order any drinks.

But sure enough, the band showed up and after they sat down, the first thing they did was order a round of drinks. I saw the look on Robert's face. He talked to them for about half an hour, gave them some tips, and never brought the subject up again.

Robert was a recovering alcoholic. He never made the point directly, though he made an indirect point by choosing who he wanted to surround him. To us, it was important to honor that. They did not, so they never heard from him again.

I checked up on these guys maybe fifteen years later and they had gone nowhere. They could have been the next Goo Goo Dolls—they were that good.

It's interesting. A person who once wanted a piece of bread changed our destiny for the better and that the same person was there, in that moment, with the band, but it didn't turn out the same way. It's all about understanding that subtle dance of dealing with people and making that first impression.

I learned that lesson well from one of our first speakers, Tone Capone. It was at our very first event. It was also when all the drama surrounding Britney Spears was on TV. Tone met with a lot of our talent, many of whom knew him because he worked with Britney. So, when people came up to him, he asked them what they thought of her. Of course, they repeated a lot of what the media said. The people didn't hold back. They said she was crazy; she was insane. She was this; she was that. Tone just replied with, "Well, do you know her?" To which all of them answered, "No."

He told them that the question was not about Britney. It was about her music. The question was asking them their opinion of her as an artist. Whether or not they loved her music, they should still respect her as an artist.

She was going through a lot, but most of the people passing judgments didn't know *her*. They only knew what they were being told. Tone knew her. So, to some extent, he understood what she was going through, versus those fresh faces who yearned for fame in the genre. But, because of public opinion, they easily and immediately threw a fellow artist under the bus.

He taught them to be very careful with their opinions because opinions are not facts. What you see on the news is rarely the whole truth. You don't want to give the wrong impression, or even the impression that you think you're better than a fellow professional, just because you see or hear something that belittles or demonizes their character.

Since then, I choose the words I use very carefully because I always want to give someone their grace, gratitude, and respect. I don't know what it's like to be them. Nor do I know what they're going through. I will not let my opinion affect my impression of them before we actually meet. In the same way, I don't want public opinion to ruin their initial impression of me.

CONNECTING THE DOTS

Being able to connect the dots is a superpower that we always have to keep working on and building up. We talk to people all the time and your mind, in the background, has to be connecting the dots. That ability comes from the habit of repetition.

Every time we have a conversation, it's like we're hunting lions and if you're not prepared, the lions are going to eat you, right? So, you can either be a lion or you can be a gazelle—you don't want to be a gazelle. You want to go into these conversations and go to these networking events, knowing who you're going to be talking to and also what the connections are to those people.

Recently, I was sitting down with Sharon Lechter, Mark Victor Hansen, and the former Attorney General of Nevada. I wound up talking to Greg Reid, the author of *Three Feet from Gold*. I had met Gregg about fourteen years before and he had given me his number. But I had never called him. So, I was "meeting him" again, only this time, with the former Attorney General.

Again, Gregg said, "Oh, here's my number." I started putting the number in my phone and realized that I'd had his number for 14 years. This led to a rather funny interaction between the three of us. Then, about a month later, the former Attorney General of Nevada was speaking at one of our events. Gregg even came to speak at our events as well.

We might have still had them speak at our events, but that connection is what I believed helped make that happen. It's always about the connection you have and knowing the connections they have.

Yes, I can throw out names and connections, but the point is once you reach a certain level of success, once you can give value to people at that higher level, then the value of what they can give back to you is always tenfold.

It all comes back to my "Why."

See, if I can get these people to come speak at our events and deliver these messages, then it will be a great experience for them—life-changing in some ways. So, if I'm not the one helping people, whether they're fresh in the industry or have been here for a while, then who will?

We always want to meet new people, but there are a few things to remember if you're looking to make *real* connections in this industry.

The first thing to do is research their most up-to-date bio. Whenever someone speaks at our events, for example, that's what we ask for. Then, start reading up on them, whether it's a Wikipedia page or something else. I love using IMDb, the internet movie database, to see what different projects someone might be working on. It's great too, because you can just search a name, then get the complete list of the cast and crew working on whatever project it might be.

While I'm doing that, I try to find what the commonalities are. For example, when I first had the chance to meet with Sigourney Weaver, I knew her from her long, illustrious career and growing up with the *Alien* movies. So many people were waiting to talk with her, but they were all saying the same things. They were saying things like, "Oh my God, I remember you in this and that," and, "I'm such a huge fan." She would smile, thank them, and move on to the next conversation. So, when I was reading up on her, I was getting to know that little bit more about her. Whether it was something about her life or something about what she was working on now. It was something that she could be excited about in the moment.

I discovered she owns a charity that provides Broadway show tickets to underprivileged children, which is such a great experience for these kids. The ticket prices can be very high. Sigourney took it upon herself to share the Broadway experience with these kids. It was something that she was really passionate about. So, when I spoke to her that night, that's what I talked about.

I thanked her for what she was doing for those kids and for sharing the magic of Broadway with them. And when I did that, she just had this really great smile. It created a commonality between the two of us, and that's what I look for, no matter who it is I'm talking to.

The lesson: Learn who people are, not just what they do or have done in the past. It's not about the awards and accolades; it's about who they are as a person. Learn about their passions and their passion projects so that you can find those commonalities because they do exist.

- And when you feel that energy and passion, you create an instantaneous connection. Your neurotransmitters in your mind start firing off and you want to learn more about them. So, when you start looking at their bio, you start seeing the paths that led them to those moments and passions. You start connecting the dots.

- I could be talking to Brad Pitt, Sylvester Stallone, Al Pacino, whoever it is, but all of a sudden, they just light up and start talking because I start asking what they're doing right now. I inquire about what I can do to help them, what I can bring to the table to help them make this mission come to fruition, to make the dream come true. It's offering and, if you're able, bringing value to their passions and the things they really care about at the moment. Just by doing that, you open up doors that you never even knew existed.

INTERVIEWS FROM THE INDUSTRY, PART ONE

Haviland Stillwell

Multi Hyphenate Actress, Singer, Producer, Director, Writer

I have a unique experience when it comes to this industry. I've navigated my way through all the corners of the entertainment industry and seen everything—the good, the bad, the ugly, and the in-between.

I've been doing this my whole life since I was a little girl. My dad is an attorney and a politician, and when I was a kid, my mom worked in the industry as a theater producer. Then she started doing more promotions, bringing large tours and concerts to my hometown, and after that, she worked in casting. So, I was always around it. In my opinion, politics, law, and entertainment are really the same thing; they need the same skill set.

Growing up, my brother and I knew we couldn't just say

or do whatever we wanted because we were a very public family, on a smaller scale, certainly not to the level of national fame and notoriety. We had a kind of awareness and picked up some of the same skills as our parents because we were exposed to those worlds. I wouldn't say either of my parents pushed me at all; I just knew. They were doing whatever it was that they wanted to do. Even as a very young child, I knew within myself that I wanted to be an "artist." I knew that that was what I was supposed to be doing before I even had the words for it.

There are so many different ways to be successful in the entertainment industry. There's an infinite number of paths to get to whatever it is that you want to be doing, and having those connections is absolutely instrumental in that. The connections that you have can help guide you to the right path or even help you to navigate the multiple paths you might be on.

Nobody does this alone. Nobody is successful, in any capacity, on their own. Even self-made entrepreneurs have had so many people help them along the way in every aspect, not just in business. But in their personal life, as well as through their family and friends. There are just so many people that are necessary to help you become successful.

For me, as a young artist, I had this idea that I was going to do it on my own. I was extremely disciplined and determined, and I actually did do a lot of it on my own. In hindsight, I can say honestly that I think I missed out on many parts of childhood and young adulthood because I was so determined to make my dreams come true. I don't necessarily think that was a bad thing. "It is what it is," as they say. But a core part of this industry is connecting.

Connections themselves are not everything. They can

help, but the whole point of art is to connect. That's what it is. It's expression and connection. I express myself through my voice, the instrument of my body, in the movement of my face. I use all of myself to deliver the message, no matter what character I'm playing or what genre or medium I'm working in. It's always about connecting with people, opening people's minds, and making them feel less alone. As much as the people that I've met along the way have been incredibly instrumental in helping me to get to the next phase, or a different phase in my career, the idea of connections and connecting is really at the core of this industry.

Jessica DiGiovanni
Actress, TV Actress Voice-Actress, Broadway Actress, Model

When it was time for me to go to college, it was kind of a no-brainer. I knew what I was going to do. I was going to perform. It was the only thing that I had ever done that made me happy, and I was fortunate enough to be able to go to school for it. A lot of people aren't that lucky, so I was very fortunate to have supportive parents and the ability to go to school to study what I loved.

My mom has said to me and my brother how lucky we are because we always knew what we wanted to do. We just gravitated pretty quickly toward what we loved. The whole trajectory has always felt right. This is definitely what I am supposed to be doing.

I went to Fordham University at Lincoln Center; that was a huge step in the right direction. I made a couple of great connections there. While I was there, I had the opportunity to study at the London Academy of Music & Dramatic Arts

CHAPTER 2 CONNECTIONS ARE KEY

(LAMDA) for a semester as well as at the Moscow Art Theater in Russia. I got a lot of experience, and I made some really great connections while in school.

For example, at Fordham, when I was doing my last show, the director's fiancée, who was also a playwright, came to one of the dress rehearsals. She was going to be doing a show at Cherry Lane, and Colin, the director, pulled me aside and said that she wanted me to audition for a part in her play. She thought I'd be perfect for it, so of course, I said yes.

I was still in school, but I auditioned for her show at Cherry Lane, and I booked it. It was crazy! I had the last dress rehearsal of my senior showcase and opening night for Cherry Lane on the same night. I did the beginning of my senior showcase and then took a cab down to Cherry Lane Theater to do my show. I was working with a playwright right after I graduated!

Another connection I made at Fordham was through the senior showcase class. The first semester, they brought in a casting director, and my casting director was Harriet Bass. They talk to you about the business, how to audition, what are good agencies, what are the casting offices, the castings that we would be right for, and all that stuff.

I had to audition for Manhattan Theater Club, but I ended up booking that role as well. That connection from Fordham with Colin opened so many doors for me. It was definitely an intimate, organic connection. They were creative people that I vibed with, who happened to be up and coming, and who liked working with me.

I am pretty good at keeping in touch with people, so I kept in touch with her for a while. She started to bring me in for things. Years ago, one of the things she brought me in for was *Bike America* which I ended up booking and doing at the Alliance Theater. It ended up going to Off-Broadway that fall.

Another one of my Fordham connections brought me in for a show that also ended up Off-Broadway, which got me one of my first agents. I developed a close relationship with Alaine Alldaffer for Playwright's Horizons.

Making real connections is about feeling out who you vibe with creatively and whose energy is on your plane. When you do it that way, it's not forced at all because there's mutual respect and affection. Things just evolved in that way for me. Because I put myself in the right places, sought to train myself with the best people and worked at what I love. I was lucky.

Jam Murphy
Wilhelmina Model, Actress

I've been modeling for over ten years, and before that, I was drawn to the excitement of a city. I was born in Ohio, found my tribe in L.A., and settled in New York—and I've been here for about a decade now. Over the past three years, I've started focusing on acting and have recently wrapped up filming my first leading role in a feature film.

When I first started, I didn't know anyone in the field. I got the name of my modeling agent after being scouted by a casting director for the show *The Biggest Loser*. I was working as a personal trainer and was invited to come onto the show to be one of their trainers. The casting director then put me in contact with my agent because they thought I would make a great sports model.

That's kind of what started the next step in that specific chapter of my life. After that, my agent was able to open me up to all these incredible brands that were hiring. It's important to connect yourself with the right people on the same level of energy and frequency. You want to have people around you that are lifting you up, helping you grow, and supporting your success. It's important to share like-mindedness, you know?

Even the chapter I'm in now was started through the connections I made. I met Tony Daniels by helping put together a charity music video because I knew the songwriter. Tony introduced me to Thomas Waites, and it was through knowing Tom, I got my first leading role in the feature film, *Target*.

I met Michael (Michael Fomkin) a little over a year ago on set for *Target*. He was instrumental in getting the film off the ground, so I'm eternally grateful for that and everything that has come with it. It was a project that gave me an artistic family, and there's even a line in the film that Tom (Thomas G. Waites) wrote, "To family, whatever the fuck that means." That's what it's like in this industry. We're all creatives in the entertainment industry. We have to find our own family, and it helps to have family members throughout the industry.

Do some networking in another avenue of art, even if you're not struggling. But if you are, it can help you find opportunities you never even knew existed. It was because I got involved in music that I got the chance to meet the right people and star in a feature film. My best friend is a singer and I like to write poetry. I would write songs with her, and I developed an interest in the industry, so I signed up for an email list to get in touch with women in music. That's how I saw the advert for the music video, and that's how I met Tony, and eventually Tom. The music industry bridged the gap for me, so go out there and make friends. Look in every corner to find your tribe and your family because they might appear where you least expect them.

Santino Fontana

Tony-Award Winning Actor, Voice of Prince Hans (Frozen, 2013), TV Actor, Broadway Actor

The summer before my senior year of high school, I went to Interlochen Arts Camp in Michigan, and it really opened my eyes. I suddenly was surrounded by a bunch of kids my age who were also doing what I liked to do and were interested in a lot of the same things I was interested in. A lot of them were even interested in pursuing it as a career, which was surprising to me. It was the first time anyone told me that if I wanted to be doing this for a living, I could.

While I was there, they were talking about a scholarship competition for high school seniors called YoungArts. Acting was one of the categories and you had to make a tape: a monologue and a song. Then, from all the tapes sent to them from all across the country, the scholarship team would pick the 20 that stood out to them. I was one of them.

They flew us to Miami, where we had a week of exercises and workshops. There were a bunch of different hoops that we had to jump through so they could gauge what we could do. Then they gave scholarship money based on that.

Miami was another step on the road with people saying, you know if you want to do this, you could do this. I met my mentor, Kenneth Washington, there. He was one of the judges. He became a really, really good friend, and my artistic mentor in a way. He was starting a new acting program in Minneapolis at the Guthrie Theater, a regional theater. I didn't even know about "regional theater" at the time, and I had no idea that people were in theater other than Broadway. I mean, I had no idea what Broadway really was either, to be honest.

At the time, I was thinking of maybe focusing on music.

He took me under his wing and stopped me; he said that I would be making a mistake. At first, I was angry at him. Then he explained that he thought I was an actor first and that I would be able to do everything that I wanted to. He thought that it would be better if I focused on training as an actor before anything else.

I trusted him, so I went to Minneapolis. I was in the first class at the Guthrie's Theater B.F.A. Actor Training Program in association with the University of Minnesota. So, I did that for an intense four years. There were no upperclassmen, we were the newbies. They called us the trail blazers, but we were the guinea pigs. We started with nineteen and we ended with fifteen. It took fifteen very, very, strong-willed, adventurous people to do something that had never been done and just see how it went! It was a huge risk.

After I graduated, I was hired as a company member at the Guthrie for a year. I was in *Death of a Salesman* and *A Christmas Carol*. I directed two things with student groups, and I was also in *As You Like It*.

At one point I moved to New York for a short period, but I got hired to go back to the Guthrie and play Hamlet. Because the University of Minnesota was supporting this professional theater, you were able to meet actors who came to Minneapolis to be in those shows. We would get to talk to them and ask them about living in New York or L.A.

I was assistant director in a John Guare play that Courtney Vance and Angela Bassett were starring in, and I was assigned to be the guy who ran lines with them on the weekend. I would go to their apartment, and I got to know them pretty well. I was there for the whole process with them. They stayed in touch with me. Courtney even came back to Minneapolis to see me in *Hamlet*.

He told me that when I came to New York he would be happy to help me out however he could, and he did. He hooked me up with my first agent when I moved there. I met the agent and auditioned for them and started working with them. A couple years ago, when I was nominated for a Tony, Courtney ended up winning a Tony that same year, and so we were both at the Tony luncheon. It was very surreal.

Relationships are everything, especially in what we do. It's a small world, and the more you work, the more likely it is that you'll end up working with people you like and connect with. I never had any specific networking plans, but I'm sure there was a part of me that was actively wanting to set up relationships with people that I admired and who were doing things similar to what I wanted to be doing.

I'm grateful that I went to an acting school first, because for what I wanted to do, I didn't want to be limited in any way. I always remember something that my mentor Ken would say to me. He said, "The world will try to limit you, don't try to limit yourself."

Alexandria De Rossi

The Firm LA Model & Talent Agent

I was at the Plaza de Oro Mall in Encino when a short character kept following us around. I was with my godsister at the time, and it concerned her so much that we went to security. Finally, Alan Benfield Bush approached me and gave me his business card, saying that he wanted me to do some hair modeling for him. And that's how I got started. I started doing hair modeling. Alan would fly me all over the place doing these amazing hair shows, and then I signed up with his agency.

I was with him for a few years, and then I decided I wanted to do more in modeling. There was a gentleman in Pasadena, Adrien William, who owned Adrien Models, and I'll never forget the first time I met him. Someone referred me to him, so I called his office, and he invited me to come to the office with a specific time to show up. He had never seen me before. I showed up not knowing what I was doing or what to expect, and he was hosting auditions. He was casting a Britannia Jean commercial and when I walked in; he threw a pair of jeans at me and just told me to try them on. I put them on and when I came out; the client liked me. The next day, I was off to Vegas to do the commercial outside of Caesars Palace. It was wild!

From there, I signed with Judith Fontaine, who booked me on *The Price is Right* as the first African American model to appear on the show. There were others later, but I was the first one to be booked. So, in a way I made history, which was just amazing.

I'm a firm believer that in this industry, even today, it's all about who you know, and being able to be in the right place at the right time. Casting directors have a major role in your career, but they all have their "go-tos," their favorites, and that's where direct booking comes in. Oftentimes, I'll get a call and it'll be a casting director enquiring if I still represent specific talent.

I think that should be every actor's goal—to get to the point where you are direct booking and bypass that audition process by being requested by casting. To do that, you have to be good at what you do. You have to be prepared, have all your tools in your toolbox, and bring your A-game each and every time—no matter the role you're auditioning for.

So many people think, *oh, I got my BFA in acting, I'm gonna be a star.* It's not as easy as that. It's work and this business can be ugly too. Statistics say that you have to go on fifty-plus auditions before you book your first big deal. It's a lot of work, a lot of patience, and a lot of no's before you get that yes. You can't give up. If you are truly passionate about your career as an actor, you can't throw in the towel. You have to keep pushing. You have to keep going.

Samuel Jackson said it best in his master class. He went on every single audition, even though he knew that he wasn't going to get paid for it, because, based on his experience, that audition opened doors that he never even expected.

Today's climate is different, though.

I've seen clients get auditions but turn down the role because they didn't think that role was right for them. But if it wasn't right for you and casting didn't think you brought what they needed to the table, then perhaps you wouldn't have been brought into the audition in the first place. You have to see the opportunity presented. I've never been an agent who would encourage or insist that clients take something that just went against their moral values, their culture, or things of that nature, but I try to encourage people to get outside of their heads. Some of the greats have done things that they can easily say they were not comfortable with, but they still brought it and aced it. You can't be afraid to step outside your comfort zone.

If you want it, you really have to go for it.

Les Brown

Motivational Speaker, Politician, Former Ohio State Representative

When I started in this industry, it was at a time that, if you were going to make it in any place, you had to face the reality that you are "nobody" unless you're standing next to "somebody."

When I was taking the leap into the speaking industry, one of the defining moments in my career was when I took a picture with Dr. Norman Vincent Peale, and he endorsed it. Dr. Peale wrote the book *The Power of Positive Thinking*. I was a "nobody," but he was a "somebody." He had been recognized as the Father of Positive Thinking; people knew him, so that inspired the question, who's that standing next to him? It was that question that actually led to a newspaper article titled "The Grand Old Master and the Young Rising Star." That was a game-changer.

So, when you think about being able to make it in an industry that has a high unemployment rate, you have to be strategic in your thinking. Branding and aligning yourself with people who are where you want to be, who are known and recognized, and who have a broader audience and reach than you is critical. When you connect with those people, what that does is that it puts your career on steroids. It saves you time. It saves you energy and effort. It gives you credibility.

I was standing before a group of people and I asked them, "If you had six months to live, what would you do differently?" I said, "I don't want you to raise your hands. I want you to ask yourself that question."

The first time I heard that question, it was jarring because what I said to myself was, "I would quit my job." I was doing something that wasn't me, and I didn't want to be doing that anymore. I think this is something a lot of people relate to, even today.

When everyone was working from home, the projection

was that around 15% of people who were told, "Okay, you can come back to the office," would say, "I don't want to do that." But the number was past 35% when it came to it. 35% of people said they didn't want to do that anymore. 35% of people said they were tired of working a job where they were being paid just enough to keep them from quitting. 35% of people said they wanted to own their life and break from that contract of mediocrity.

So, ask yourself, what are you doing? Is what you are doing right now what you want to be doing and is it *you*? Once you get clear on that, the next step is to decide on a compelling reason to go for it. You need to find something that means you will not give up and you will not stop because your reason will make you unstoppable. Your reason is what makes you persevere.

When you look at Finding Fame, you need to do just that. I teach people to live their life the way that *they* want to lead their life. I have a principle that I've been teaching for years: O.Q.P - Only Quality People. You can tell who the quality people are because of the impact they're able to make with their lives. My prayer is constantly, "Lord, help me to live a life that will outlive me," because I want my life to have an impact in this world.

There's a story I love about Leonard Nimoy and Robert Kennedy. When Leonard worked driving cabs in New York, Robert was one of the passengers he picked up. He was telling Robert about how he was pursuing a career as an actor and felt that he had a lot of talent, but he wasn't getting the recognition or the opportunities he felt he should get. He was discouraged and felt like he should just give up, but before Robert got out of that cab, he said, "Don't give up. They always make room for the great ones."

Leonard went on to say that that one trip was the defining moment in his career, and that is the impact that I want to be able to have on people. I want to inspire them and keep inspiring them long after I'm gone.

Having someone who believes in you until your belief in yourself kicks in, can make all the difference. Having that connection, relationship, introduction, or experience with someone who is where you want to be or who sees something in you that you can't see in yourself can be your defining moment.

Robert Funaro

The Sopranos (2001-2006), Actor, TV Actor

Networking is important; it's so important. The Streetcar show I did with Jimmy (James Gandolfini) was very important. If I'd never answered that backstage call or if I'd decided I didn't need to do it, my life would have never been as great as it is. If I hadn't done that call, I'd never have had the chance to work on *The Sopranos* and to work with such a genius like James Gandolfini.

Once you learn your craft, once you've done your two years of study and continued onward, once you've got your base, go out and work no matter what. Don't refuse any jobs, just go out there and work and meet people. And life is funny because it seems like you're on the bottom or the top, but it's circular.

If you stay within the circle, in the network of people, the circle keeps turning, and all of a sudden you realize that you're on the top of the circle, and then, of course, you start going down. Everything in life kind of fades, or maybe it doesn't fade; maybe you're one of the fortunate people who never see it fade. But the circle is going to turn and if you stay in it long enough, if you keep playing the game, you never know what might happen. So networking is essential.

VIP Ignite connects you with people and professionals, and they try to be as truthful as they can be. They choose the professionals that talk to talent so that their talent has the best possible shot at making it in the industry. It's not easy but knowing the right people and doing the right things makes it seem less impossible. You definitely need that base of learning your craft, but I've said it on the stage at VIP Ignite events: try to get into a two-year training program as an actor.

If you're a person who doesn't know much about acting, I would look into an acting program. I really wouldn't try to approach directors and other actors until you have some sort of base. Learn the work first; learn the great writers; and have fun while you're doing it. Then after that, you want to work as much as possible for people to see you. You want to network for people to see you.

Find a niche for yourself, but to be honest with yourself, too. You don't want to be doing something you don't enjoy just because that's what you think you want to do. If something else actually takes your interest, go and pursue that thing instead. Even if it's writing or lighting, or something you never thought of before, go for it. After you find that out, others will approach you. People will recognize you for your talents. Then you can run with the best runners in that race.

Everyone has to start somewhere. Some people start at the top and they work their way down, then they work their way up again—but you've got to start somewhere. It's important to know that it is a process of starting somewhere and gradually getting to where you want to be. It's good to know about other people and how they broke in. I wish I had read more biographies before I started. There are a lot of them out there. You should be reading voluminously about other people's careers.

I don't think acting can be taught. I think it just needs to be "directed." It's training someone, pointing them in the right direction. You want to place yourself in a fertile place where you can grow. A lot of times that is with your colleagues and producing your own stuff.

Thomas G. Waites
Director, Producer, Writer

One summer I worked on the railroad swinging a sledgehammer. I wanted to be an actor, and nothing was going to stop me. So, if I had to get a job on the railroad, well then Goddamnit, that's what I did.

I had a roommate who was, more often than not, stoned out of his mind, but he used to brag about the fact that his dad was the head of Penn Central in Colorado and that he was really good friends with the head of Penn Central on the East Coast. I was like, "Oh yeah? Well, what's his name?" He then tells me the guy's name; I look up the number and call the guy.

I say that I'm a friend of Rick Warbles from Colorado and he reminisces, saying that any friend of Rick's is a friend of his. So I go, "I got two guys, they're needing jobs this summer. Can you help us out?" And he told me to send them round tomorrow. That was back in the middle 70s and we were making around $12-14 an hour, which would be like $90-100 an hour today. So, for an eighteen-year-old kid, that was really good. It was awesome, and I did it because I'm an actor and I was able to create a relationship, a connection.

That experience didn't have anything to do with being on Broadway or making a name for myself, which I eventually did, but it taught me humility. That experience of working in the Bronx, going to 149th Street and Mott Avenue, working there with those people, and being around the real people in the Bronx, taught me who I was. More importantly, it taught me the value of friendship because, really, that's the core of this industry.

Going through the movies that I've been in, the plays I've been in, even the productions I've been a part of, I can't tell you the number of times when I'd be sitting at the conference table surrounded by the directors and producers, and they've said, "Okay, we need someone for this role, who can you think of?" Immediately I think of my friends, and then I go through who would be best for the part.

If you have those relationships, then you'll always be near the top of the list because people like working with you, but it doesn't always mean you'll get the call. For example, I could be doing a play, and someone drops out. My first thought is why don't we get Christine Estabrook, she'd be great in that part.

How does that happen?

It happens in your acting class, because, before we even get the relationships, we have to have a craft and a technique, right? You have to know how to act, just like how a musician needs to be able to play their instrument. If I pick up a guitar, I have to know what a 145 progression means. I have to know how to play a Blues progression. I have to know what D to F# minor to A to C# minor to F# minor to E major means. I have to know what that progression means or I'm not a musician, right?

In the same way, an actor must know speech, voice,

diction, text, meaning, and language. Then, of course, there's your body. You have to constantly be working on your body. You have to make your body a flexible, pliable, malleable instrument that expresses your emotion. And finally, and most importantly, you have to have command of your emotions. You have to be able to laugh and or cry on the spot. If you cannot do these things, you have not been trained, and you really have no business networking or making friends or doing anything else until you've mastered these tools.

Bill Walsh

CEO of PowerTeam International, America's Small Business Expert, Top Success Coach, Top Business Coach, Author

When you're around people that live what they teach, getting to where you want to be, wherever that might be, becomes a lot easier. But if they're just talking about it and not living it, that's a pattern disconnect. You don't want that. You want to be with people who live in the industry in real time. People who are in the here and now, not just 25 years ago, that's how you learn about what's happening in the industry NOW.

In this business, it's not just who you know; it's who knows you. When you're around people that are doing some cool stuff, you need to be the first one to get the check at dinner. You're gonna make yourself instantly memorable. And the fun part about it is, that when you get around some of those right connections, they can open up doors that you could never open up in 20 years on your own, just by making one phone call or one text message.

You've heard that it's "six degrees of separation." Well, the truth is, it's only two. You are two people away from anyone. But you've got to be the one to step up and say, "Here are the folks I need to connect with. Here are the people I'd love to learn more about."

I always believe when you meet people, "it's for a reason, a season, or a lifetime." There are no accidents. So, when you meet certain people, they have the ability to open doors that can change your life. BUT when those doors are opened, you have to be the one to walk through them.

90% of success is showing up. You have to show up for your own success story.

There are a lot of people who will say, "It's not going to work." Even when they have the greatest opportunity of their lives in front of them, they will not show up because they've been conditioned to think that no matter what they do or try, it won't happen. Those are the people who make excuses. They are the people who can't attend an event because they've got to look after the dog or who can't invest in that training opportunity because they're already busy that week. If this is something you want to do, you will make it happen; you won't make excuses.

Make zero time for people in your life who make excuses. Instead, put yourself in the right place, talk to the people who are where you want to be, and listen to and learn from the conversations that will add value to your life.

Listen, learn, process, and whatever you promise, deliver on it. If you want to keep those connections, you have to follow up and follow through. Follow up and follow through on everything you say you're going to do, whether it's for yourself or someone else.

Scott Patrick Erwin

Actor, Model, Writer

The connections that I have made have been inspirational to me.

When you're going through the disciplines that are required to get ready and be ready for an acting career, oftentimes, having the right mental mindset and perspective is challenging. Having those connections and having that encouragement is invaluable because, by networking, you have those people that you can look to, reach out to, and ask for advice. It's very useful and so helpful.

I'll give you an example. I had written a book that was really just a book of essays. I had an acting coach, Robert Galinsky, who suggested that I turn the essays into monologues. He thought they told an interesting story, so he suggested that I shorten them, make a character, and retell them from a different perspective. I ended up making monologues and turned them into a short series on YouTube.

It's something that I may not have thought of. In fact, I never would have thought of that idea. I wrote something and thought it stood alone. Then Robert came along and recommended something else. It's advice that I wouldn't have gotten had I not been connected with him. It did take me a while to come up with the character, but eventually, I found the right one and it was a lot of fun.

Getting advice from the people that have actually been there, done that, and who are still doing it in the industry makes such a big difference.

CHAPTER 3

THE TRUTH OF THE INDUSTRY

There are two sides to the entertainment industry. There is the fun, glitzy, and glamorous side that appears on the covers of magazines and the red carpets of film and theater. But there is also a darker side, though not quite as dark as some of the common misconceptions that surround the industry would have you believe, like you'll be scammed, kidnapped, sold off, and never heard from again. That side does exist. Stories come out all the time of the abuse and mistreatment of actors, musicians, and models, but more commonly the dark side of the industry is not at this level.

A DARKER SIDE TO THE ONLINE WORLD

In today's market, also years ago, there are a lot of scam companies, but unlike back then, they are a lot more organized than they once were. They used to have physical offices, flashy videos, fake sponsors, and promotional material. They had to work hard to make everything look legitimate, but that's not quite the case anymore. Most scam companies today don't have physical offices; most aren't even located in the United States anymore. There are still some, but there is a larger percentage of them that are located overseas, and almost all of them utilize social media to engage with potential clients. It's so simple.

I can go on Instagram and create a modeling agency. I just need an email. Then I can go on Instagram, open up an account, steal other models' pictures, and put them up on my Instagram account. I can create the facade of an agency and start direct messaging people promoting this new agency, looking to fly them out to London, or offering them a shoot in New York in the hopes of hooking them.

Now, no legitimate agency reaches out to you on your Instagram saying we're going to book you for a job, but there's an excitement that is often experienced by the new talent that blinds them to the con. An agency reaches out to them, offering a $5,000 check for featuring them in a magazine, but they first have to pay $500 for the photographer because they are overseas. They take the job and suddenly money starts getting passed back and forth, funded and refunded, and then, of course, the final check bounces, and they're gone. The aspiring talent is $1,000, $2,000, even $5,000, out of pocket with the so-called agency vanishes. It's something that seems outlandish, but it happens. They target newcomers to the industry, and for some of these scams, they take it one step further. They target young people, putting them in compromising positions to extort money from them.

The problem with the online world is how do you stop it? You can make an Instagram account just as fast as the site can take it down. The accounts are put up, they're taken down, and then within a few hours, another one appears. It's the same thing on Twitter and Facebook, with some even moving into TikTok as its popularity continues to grow. Anywhere that has the potential to grow and influence has the potential for scammers. They appeal to their naivety and their vanity, anything they can, to get them to let their guard down.

I've been doing this for so long that I've seen the same scams time and time again in various forms and on different platforms. There are always people who'll take advantage when they think they can and there's always people who try to make something from nothing. I think this is something that will always remain part of the industry. It's one of the reasons that I advise people never to get involved in anything without understanding the business or even researching it, making sure that you understand the mechanics of it.

- How do you break it down?

- How do you navigate it?

- How does it *really* work?

In this industry, every part is connected. From the businesses to the agencies, from the scouts to the talent, the whole business is interconnected.

For example, the company Johnson and Johnson is looking to hire a female model in her mid-thirties to be in a new advert for Johnson's Baby. But imagine if Johnson and Johnson just started reaching out randomly on Instagram. They're looking for a model who can fill the role of the mom, so they contact a woman, who, from her posts, interactions, and photographs, appears to fit perfectly, about the opportunity to be a part of their advertisement. She accepts, stars in the advert, and is now the face of Johnson's Baby. However, unknown to the company, the woman they're now affiliated with had just been released from prison only a few weeks before, after being charged with abusing children. Now everyone who sees that advert has the potential to recognize that woman as a convicted felon, a convicted fraud. How would that make the Johnson and Johnson brand look?

Now, this is arguably an unlikely example, but there is always a chance of the unlikely happening. It is why agencies exist in the first place; to source credible, honest people that are right for the job. It is why there are so many connections in the industry because people need to know who you are. Nobody is reaching out to you on the internet because they have no idea who you are. They want people who are going to show up on time, people who know what they're doing, and they want a level of certainty that they'll get these things when they hire talent. Clients, brands like Johnson and Johnson, go through agencies because agencies vet their talent.

The client expects you to have a certain level of industry understanding and knowledge; it's not the responsibility of the agency to teach you what to do once you're in front of the camera. It's called the entertainment business because it is there to entertain people but, at the end of the day, it is still a business. Anybody looking to work in the industry should always keep that fact present in their mind.

Clients often pay a lot of money for a modeling shoot, an advert, or a ten-second jingle, and they expect quality results because if not, it affects more than just the brand. The success of the brand affects every person working for that brand, it affects lives and livelihoods as well as profits. When you take a contract, you become the face, or the sound of that brand and you've got to know what you're doing. Most clients will not hire someone who's brand new, and most agencies wouldn't recommend someone who's brand new for certain jobs. That means that certain routes are automatically inaccessible to those who are just starting in the industry. The question then becomes, if you're the talent, not the agency or the client, how do you get people to vouch for you? How do you get work if you're lacking experience?

I truly believe that everyone has to start somewhere; everybody has to be given a chance. VIP Ignite, I'd like to believe, is the place where people can start. We give you the experience that agencies are looking for and the knowledge that clients want. We will help you understand how the acting, modeling, and music industries work because we don't simply bring on acting coaches or talent scouts. We get you on stage, on shoots, and in front of cameras to perform and learn. Everything we try to do, that I want VIP Ignite to do for new talent, becomes part of a resume that appeals to agencies.

FINDING THE RIGHT AGENT

What do you do if you have the right knowledge and you're starting to build your resume? The clients are not going to contact you, so do you start contacting them?

I won't say that this is a bad way of doing things. For some people, this was how they got their break into the industry. They were persistent, took a chance, and found success by continuously reaching out to experts in the industry. However, it's not something I would advise.

When you're on your own, you have to be both the talent and the agent. Even as you start to develop your knowledge of the industry and build your skills, you're always going to be competing with people who have more experience than you and dealing with people who have more knowledge than you.

It can be difficult trying to juggle your career by yourself and it's hard to know what is really in your best interest.

Today everyone knows about the scandal involving Harvey Weinstein that started in October 2017, with a story published in the New York Times. The Times story detailed decades of allegations of sexual harassment that continued to spiral and escalate until Weinstein was convicted in March 2020 on several accounts of rape and sexual assault.

The whole process exposed a darker side to the industry, especially for aspiring young women who were looking for their big break from the 70s right through to the early 2000s. Court records showed that through horrid forms of manipulation, Weinstein convinced these women that he held the keys to their careers and that if they didn't comply with his demands, he had the power to ensure they would never succeed in the industry.

During the periods when the allegations were being made, a lot of those women were trying to navigate the industry by themselves. They were so scared and trusting of people who knew more about it than they did; they became stuck in that world, believing they didn't have another option. They needed to succeed.

Things have changed, attitudes have changed, and there are more policies and rules in place to protect people in the industry now. That's not to say that there are not people out there still who are looking to take advantage of young and new talent.

You want to have someone on your side who can look out for you. You want someone who has that industry experience and knowledge to know what's best for your career and know when something is in your best interest. That's the role of an agent.

They are there to find you opportunities that will develop your skills and build your resume, but a good agent will also communicate with you, be open with you, advise you, and protect you against situations that would take advantage of you. It's why we always say that you need an agent. Your agent is the person who's talking on your behalf; they're the ones negotiating with clients and putting your name forward.

But the next question is, how do you know whether or not an agent is legitimate?

There are signs you can look for when searching for an agent to represent you; things that, when we teach new talent, we tell them to keep an eye out for, even if they think an agent is 100% legitimate. Just like clients contacting you directly through your social media, an agent contacting you directly through Instagram, TikTok, or even Facebook, should usually be red flagged for questioning the legitimacy of their offer.

A legitimate agency is not going to contact you through social media or put up adverts looking for models because they don't need to look for models. Models come to them and from that, they can be very selective about who they're going to work with. It's not like an open call when anyone can show up, so everyone shows up. With the internet, if agencies were to try this method, they'd have hundreds, maybe even thousands, of potentials showing up looking to get hired and it becomes a waste of time and money to only hire a handful from the massive line-up.

So, what if you are the one to try and contact them? How do you know that who you're contacting is really legitimate?

First off, most legitimate agents are listed on the SAG-AFTRA franchised agents list. Via their website, you can search for well-known and reputable agencies that are local to you, giving you their contact information and specialties to see if they will be able to effectively represent you.

Another thing you can check for is if they have any memberships like SAG-AFTRA, or if they are a part of the CSA, the Casting Society of America. You can search for casting directors and associates from across the world as well as specific castings for the likes of TV, film, theater, commercials, and other genres in the entertainment industry. It is an incredibly useful tool for finding people who are specialized in your qualifications and attributes that can help you excel in your career.

You can see if a lot of these places are legitimate through a quick Google search. For example, do they have a legitimate website that is up to date and updated regularly, or do they have an official office space and address that, when you cross-check it, leads you to a legitimate office instead of the middle of nowhere? And even then, if all this checks out and they seem legitimate, then do some more research and use IMDb.

IMDb is great. It is the Internet Movie Database, and when you look up anything to do with the entertainment industry. It shows you a track record of everything that person or company has done within the industry. Movies and TV shows, actors and actresses, songwriters and scriptwriters, producers and directors, you name it, and you can likely find it on IMDb. It is one of the greatest tools at your disposal because if an agency is dropping names like Disney, HBO, and Netflix on their resume, then you can check that by searching for them on the IMDb system. If they're legitimate and honest, then those connections will be listed in their credits, but if they're not listed, then it's more likely that they are less than legitimate.

When you're starting out, trying to contact the big names can be difficult. A lot of them don't want to take on new talent;

they want you to have already made a name for yourself before they even consider representing you. So where do you go to make that name?

Well, that's why you look at local agencies, you start with the smaller market. You'll still be able to find results for them on these databases, they might just not have as big names attached to them. It might instead be a local law firm doing an advertising campaign that does their casting through the agency, or maybe they have credits tied to a local cable company that could get you a few small opportunities to appear on TV or online commercials.

Taking that little extra bit of time to do your research and seeing what is going on can really help you succeed in this industry. Results speak for themselves. I've had agencies get offended when I don't want to work with them. But if they don't have the credibility and the legitimacy, then that's a risk. I then need to see something special to convince me that they are worth that risk because I can go online and search for them. I can see what successes they've had on their website, see their current credits on IMDb, or even just look at their social media, and from there I can tell whether or not I want to take that risk and work with them, especially if they're a newer or smaller name.

However, that's for me. I already work in this business. I can be particular about who I work with, and that might not be the same for you. What this research can do for you is to give you a foot in the door by letting you know what kind of up-and-coming projects might be looking for cast members.

Searching for the New Mexico Film Board, for example, can show you some film titles that you don't even recognize because they might still be in production. You can then search those titles on IMDb which will list the current cast and crew, including casting directors. Then you can follow that up and try to put yourself forward, using the knowledge you have learned to submit yourself for a specific role, or type of role, as well as putting forward your resume.

Now, all this can sound a little bit overwhelming, from trying to find a legitimate agency to trying to find legitimate work. But that's why I say you should only be doing the first leg of the work and finding yourself an agent.

When you have an agent, they do everything else for you. They do the research and do the legwork to find roles and opportunities that are legitimate. And more importantly than that, there is a higher chance of casting directors responding to an agent than they would if you contact them yourself. An agent is beneficial because they are there to help you, and really there's nothing wrong with getting help. More often than not, you will get a lot further in this industry when you have people helping you.

There's nothing wrong with someone helping you get pictures or someone helping you set up your website. Just like there's nothing wrong with somebody helping you hire people for your business. But the people who help you should always be professional, credible, and most importantly upfront with you.

Actors, models, and musicians who are newcomers to the industry get tricked all the time. Extra fees for extra pictures that they promise you need or you need a little extra training to make sure you're properly prepared for this role. No matter what part of the industry you're trying to find your footing with, there are always people who are ready and willing to take advantage of you. They do it by appearing more knowledgeable and then add those additional fees.

We have full transparency with the talent that we

represent. We want to give them the skills, knowledge, and understanding to thrive in the industry. I even have a whole presentation talking about agents and casting—how you can spot a legitimate agent over a fake one as well as how you can recognize a real casting versus a fake one. These are things that at VIP Ignite we strive to do.

For our talent, we offer even more transparency through our organization Truth Management. By working with us, our talent knows exactly what their billing is, and they are in complete control of their schedule. There is a darker side to the entertainment business that so many people get wrapped up in, but VIP Ignite gives our talent a helping hand and a way to feel safe in the industry they're working in.

INTERVIEWS FROM THE INDUSTRY, PART TWO

Michael Stonewall Beaudry
Casting Director

I find most of the people I work with through my contacts, primarily through agencies, but when I first started, the bulk of them were through social media because I was trying to get people who would be great in projects. When you start, you're calling in favors when you're asking people to audition for stuff. There are "no money" jobs, and agents will see your stuff on casting boards and not submit because they don't know who the hell you are.

But as you get bigger and bigger, you start doing more and more jobs, then the money for talent starts getting bigger.

Agencies start submitting more and more, and you start going through them more and more. It's more convenient, the talent options are better, and it's also safer. The people agencies take on are vetted, so you know what you're getting when you go through their submissions.

Some of the jobs get incredibly specific as well. There have been plenty of times when I put out a breakdown for a role and only got a dozen submissions after days, for example, because the client wants somebody who speaks a certain language and is a certain gender in a certain age group. Then there are other times when I've done roles and within half an hour, I have 2,500-3,000 submissions. It gets crazy.

When you're the talent, doing the job search, looking at all these roles, whether that's through an agency or not, it's good to look up the casting directors. Go to their website, look at their credits and casting boards. Look at them over the course of a couple of months because even the biggest casting directors on the planet might not be working for a few weeks, maybe even a few months. You'll be able to find something to their credit even if they're a film student just getting out of school, trying to become a casting director. I've not really come across anyone who is pretending to be a casting director.

I think there's a lot of people out there, mostly acting coaches, who love to promise stuff to get new talent into their programs, projects, workshops, whatever it might be, and they can't guarantee what they promise. I never want to be involved with someone or something that just rips people off and I think a lot of the time that's what these people do.

I was invited to VIP Ignite by one of my directors, though she was a photographer at the time. They wanted a casting director at one of their events, so she hit me up and I trusted her, so I went along. I liked everyone the minute I met them. I just had a good feeling about everyone there. It was very good fun, and I did it again and again.

With VIP Ignite, *I saw a system that was what it was supposed to be*; there was no ulterior motive. They were, and are, helping to provide people with the tools, skill sets, confidence, and passion to get out there and chase their dreams with that extra helping hand.

Fuji Ruiz

Senior Agent, One Model Management

I've stumbled onto talent, and talent has reached out to me. I think I'll advise you on how to reach out to an agent in general. Different agencies have online submission forms that you can view. A lot have open calls and a lot of times there're some places that you can hashtag. But I think for most agencies, just do your research. Go online or call an agency and do your legwork if they have open calls. It's not looking at what address can I send my pictures to, it's about what can I do right now to improve myself and my skills.

If you're not in a big city, look up a local agency in Ohio that could help you get your foot in the door. A lot of the talent comes from small, local agencies that we work with. We already have these relationships with people across the country or in other parts of the world. They submit their talent to us, and we say yes or no or maybe. That's how we see a lot of our talent.

Yes, some are a scam and are a little weird, but then others really are legitimate placement agencies that book and place models, but I think it goes back to research. There are people that pretend to be me and my friends and stuff like that. You have to be careful. If someone tells you that they work for an agency, then do your research. Ask questions, even call the company afterward to see if they really are affiliated with them or not.

We're not completely unreachable. We do have to set a certain bar or else we'd be on the phone all day. The key for any emerging talent is always going to be: have an agency, no matter how small, just for protection. They can help and advise, and they'll help you build your career. It all goes back to what I said about relationships and networking. When I send you to events, I'm not sending you to any events for the free gift bag or the trends. I'm sending you there to be seen. I'm sending you there as another opportunity for you to meet with people and connect. Agencies help you connect.

Networking is something that no matter what you do, it's part of life. In one form or another, it helps to know another person because sometimes you might be the best at something, but this other person happens to know a lot of people. So, it's absolutely crucial, and it's part of the model career. It's making those relationships and always making new ones. It's always going to be a part of your career.

CHAPTER 4

THE RECIPE FOR SUCCESS

To me, having relationships is like having money in the bank.
You can continue to make deposits
so that the relationships grow,
or you can be needy and demanding.
You can be selfish in that your needs must be met
and your needs are the priority,
but you end up being a taker,
never looking to deposit anything.
If you're doing this, if you're constantly withdrawing,
you'll go bankrupt.
– *Alexandria De Rossi*

When casting directors, talent scouts, and people who work with new talent talk about what they're looking for, they often speak about an almost indefinable quality. Some call it "star quality," others say that it's having a sense of "stage presence," but either way, it is the elusive "it" factor that only a few seem to possess. Breaking into the industry can seem impossible for so many hopefuls simply because they don't meet that magical criterion. Most people, especially those in the industry, don't know how to properly define what "it" is, but they still look for it when they search for new talent.

If you are new or even struggling to gain traction in the industry, you can often feel lost in the crowd. It can feel overwhelming, confusing, and at times discouraging and disempowering when you face rejection after rejection and start thinking it's because you don't have the "it" factor. Being able to succeed in this industry is not about inborn, innate talent or "star quality" despite what some might think. It's about getting your skill set and confidence to the level where you can walk into an audition and the casting director can tell, just by looking, that you have what it takes. It's about honing and polishing your craft until a producer can tell from your demo tape that you've got a hit song. It's about learning to be so comfortable in front of a camera that a modeling agent picks you right out of an open call.

Building a career in the industry starts long before you get your big break; it starts with you. It starts the moment you decide you want to step across the threshold with the determination that it takes to be ready for that big break when it comes.

Actors, models, musicians, and other talents in the entertainment industry don't start their careers with a big break. Being discovered by a casting director or producer while working the front counter of a coffee shop or while busking on the street corner is something that only really happens in old Hollywood movies.

It's not impossible, though. I know people who got a chance

thanks to a random encounter and now have very successful careers. But that big break, if you ever get the chance to have one, is more likely to come after years of working and dedication, through studying your craft, making connections, and taking every step possible to move your career forward. So, what are those steps you need to take to improve your craft and career, and who are those connections you need to make?

There are different tactics for getting into the different parts of the industry. How you handle a modeling career, for example, is differs from how you would handle an acting career or a career as a musician. However, there is a point where the underlying foundations for those careers are all identical.

If you want to be a great musician, you need to understand the foundations of music. Just like if you want to be a great actor, you need to understand the foundations of characterization. You might want to be a soul musician or a rock musician, but to be successful, you need to have a deeper understanding than that one genre of music. You need to appreciate modes outside of your desired genre because only then will you have the flexibility and adaptability to compose, play, and stand alongside the greats. You might have a style you prefer, or you might have a specific role in mind or a product you want to represent. But when you start, your mindset shouldn't be *I want to be a rock musician.* It should be *I want to be a musician.*

I've lost count of how many times new talent comes to us with the drive of, "I want to be famous," "I want to be a star in Hollywood," or "I want to be on the cover of magazines," and time and time again, they're at the start of their journeys. Around 90% of our talent started with this mentality. They've spent tens of thousands of dollars on their dreams, hoping to get famous, but have little to nothing to show for it. Yet when they join us at VIP Ignite and come to our boot camps, they've suddenly gotten more out of an eight-hour session or a two-day event than they have out of years of struggling to find a way by themselves.

VIP APPROVED

From a business standpoint, it probably doesn't make a lot of sense that we put so much time and effort into new talent. It would probably be more beneficial for us to operate more like clients and agencies and work with people who are more experienced or who already have a name in the industry. I think our drive to help and support new talent all goes back to a loss of innocence.

In the online world, people can remain anonymous. If they want to see someone or something become successful, then they also have the power to disempower and destroy it. In the beginning, that's what it was like for us. We got a lot of heat; we got a lot of pushback. We got a lot of hate from people we had never met just because we put ourselves out there and people didn't understand what we were doing.

However, the risk isn't exclusive to the online world. Before VIP Ignite, when I worked as a franchisor, I trusted Lou Pearlman and that backfired as he took advantage of the company. There are always people who will try to disempower you and those who look to take advantage of you because you're new.

Another example I can give is my daughter. When she was young, she wanted to be a part of the industry and work as a model, but we never pursued it. I often think about what would have happened if I had tried to get her into the industry back then. I didn't understand the industry. I didn't know the business and I would have been one of those parents who took their kid to one of those scam places, and I would have been scammed.

No matter which way I look at it, I always put myself in those shoes. I think about how it would have felt as a parent and remember how it felt when it all went wrong with the franchise. I looked at my own experiences and decided that no one else should have to experience that. I wanted to fight on the right side, so to speak, helping those people who are brand new, those fresh faces with incredible talent who don't really know anything about the industry they want to succeed in.

So many people who have come to work with us have been beaten and battered. They were taken advantage of. They sold their songs, danced the dance, attended photoshoot after photoshoot, and forked out for classes that were not what they were promised. VIP Ignite is there to guide and protect the people who want to work and thrive in this industry.

But there is another reason I like to focus on those who are looking for their footing in this industry. Over the years, I've developed my understanding of what it takes to go from being brand new to being successful. To me, it's kind of like when I worked in the restaurant industry.

When I worked in the restaurant, the thing I enjoyed most was walking into the kitchen, seeing all the different, fresh ingredients, and creating a dish out of them. It was one of my favorite things about the job, and despite working in a completely different environment now, there are still times when I don't feel like my job has changed that much. I even give presentations I've dubbed the Actor's Cookbook and the

Model's Cookbook, where we discuss the similarities between cooking and entertainment.

Let me try to explain.

If I gave you a cake recipe and told you to bake it right now, and I did the same thing, in the end we'd have different cakes. Even though we followed the exact same recipe, our cakes wouldn't taste the same and there's a chance it wouldn't even look the same when it came out of the oven. That's because we're in different places with different brands of ingredients, and a collection of other little variances that will alter the outcome in ways we don't really think about. To get something to match, you have to follow the recipe with as few variances as possible. There's an order to it, right?

So, coming into this industry and being a part of VIP Ignite, I see myself as a chef for models, actors, musicians, and budding talent in the entertainment industry. I've learned all I can, and there's still more to learn, but I think with the path I walked and the connections I've made, I can help newcomers perfect the recipe. What I've enjoyed most about working in this industry is helping people with little to no experience because you can really see them grow.

Sometimes when you are working with people who have a lot of experience and they're failing, it's hard to get through to them and get them to change their ways. They received so much bad advice, they are stuck in their mindsets, believing that the next bit of advice they're going to get is just like all the stuff that's come before. I've gotten better at working with these people, getting them to stop and think about what is keeping them from progressing. I try to show them what isn't working and explain what they could change to get it to start. But most times, I'm still fighting a losing battle.

That's why I have so much excitement when I get to work

CHAPTER 4 - THE RECIPE FOR SUCCESS

with new people. I get to give them a safe space to experience the industry and guide them to success. Because new people have the mindset and willingness to listen, learn, and adapt in order to strengthen their knowledge, understanding, and skill set for thriving in this wild world.

INTERVIEWS FROM THE INDUSTRY, PART THREE

Deneen White
Chief Inspiration Officer, VIP Ignite, President of Talent Services, Talent Management

Pineapples. What do they have to do with modeling and acting?

Well, you know what? Sometimes this industry seems hard and prickly, but that's only on the outside. Once you go through the prickly outside, there's such sweetness on the inside, and that's what your career can be like with VIP Ignite.

There are so many things that our clients and students learn with us. One of them is mindset because it's just like a pineapple again. If you have a pineapple, it's tough, it's hard, it's prickly, but if you're not persistent and don't cut through that thick skin, then you can't get to the sweetness inside. That's why we focus on helping our clients and students develop that mindset so that they can get to the sweetness that lies beneath.

When it comes to mindset, we have amazing speakers, like Marjah Simon, who come to our events and talk about what you need to do to just take that next step in your life and your career. It's the small little things that our talent learns, and what I've found is that when they learn these different skills, it adds up and adds up and adds up.

But that's not everything. You need to have the right skill set as well as the right mindset. VIP Ignite helps you get that and so much more because we also give you connections and contacts as well. For example, we did an event recently where our talent had the opportunity to work with 50 Cent's acting coach. They got to learn about how to build chemistry on stage and off stage, in character and out of character. It was amazing! And it's something that maybe a local acting coach wouldn't really teach, but those are things you need to learn to get on a set. These are things that we offer.

Those who work with us are not only learning how to memorize lines or how to show up on set, but they're also getting so many different skills that will make them pop against all the other talent that is on set with them. They get the opportunity to network with people that maybe they wouldn't even connect to the entertainment industry, which is pretty amazing. They have the opportunity to hear and work with them and take those nuggets that they have been given and go out there and apply them in their career. When they have all this knowledge and all of these skills, they get to see themselves grow in confidence, and all of a sudden, the opportunities start coming!

So, I think it's worth getting through the prickliness because, in the end, the pineapple is pretty sweet if you ask me.

Alycia Kaback
Broadway and TV Producer, co-founder of VIP Ignite

Entitlement is the biggest, dirtiest word in this business.

That's when somebody feels that because they put money and time into things or because they think they're great, other people have to feel the same way.

Sometimes people will come in and tell me that they've already spent money on classes and photos and that they've already got all they need so they're not spending money on anything more. First, that's the wrong attitude. Second, what these people don't understand is that lessons and classes cannot "discriminate" because they're a business. It's not going to benefit these companies if they turn away money just because someone is a brunette or has freckles.

However, when you step into the world of entertainment, when you go to auditions, suddenly they *can* "discriminate" and if you don't have "it" they'll turn you away. A lot of the time it's got nothing to do with the schools or the classes. They're not scams; they're giving these people the skills they need to get started. The problem is that the people come in and think that because they spent money on classes, they're entitled to greatness.

Take the modeling industry, for instance. I, myself, am 5'4", size eight. I could take all the dance classes I wanted. I could learn how to walk like a model. I could learn how to sing, and I could learn how to play piano. I could be primed and ready to go if someone asked, but if I'm not what they're looking for, then it doesn't matter what I've got because they'll choose the woman who fits the image they need for the shoot, right?

It's not fair, but it's business.

Alexandria De Rossi
The Firm LA Model & Talent Agent

Honestly, those actors that are "seasoned," are worse than

the new faces, as far as I'm concerned, because they think they've mastered their craft.

I require all my clients to have a thirty-five to forty-second "slate" reel. It's like a personality-type reel that tells casting who you are. It tells them where you've trained, the types of roles you book, and what kind of skills you bring to the table. In my opinion, it gives casting an idea of whether or not you're an ideal fit with the rest of the cast they're selecting, as well as an ideal fit for the role. And it's so simple.

It's a short reel saying something like, "Hi, my name is Alexandria De Rossi. I'm represented by the Firm LA Model & Talent Agency. I'm Meisner trained, I have my BFA in acting, and I play the role of the girl-next-door, the mom, and the serial entrepreneur . . ." And you end it with something quirky that really speaks to your personality.

That, accompanied with your demo reel, gives you a bit of an edge and could pique the interest of casting even more, helping you increase your chances of getting called into the room. It says to casting, "Here I am and here's what I bring to the table." But for seasoned actors, sometimes, it's like pulling teeth to get them to do this.

Some of the more experienced talent have this preconceived notion that, since they've already been acting and they already have a demo reel, they don't need a slate reel. They think that a slate reel is for newcomers that don't have any experience. But their demo reel may not necessarily speak to the casting director, there's a chance that when they watch it, they don't see what they need to see. I feel like submitting your demo reel along with the slate reel gives them a little more. It lets them see you and get a feel for how you could fit into their cast.

You cannot assume that just because you're booking and you're making connections, that you know everything there is to know about this business. Things change. The climate changes.

I don't watch a lot of television. I love and prefer to watch movies, but I will force myself to watch television because I'm booking clients on TV shows. Everything right now is sex, to the point that it's almost pornographic. The climate has changed quite a bit because you don't see a lot of wholesome, family-oriented TV anymore. So, you've got to continue to perfect your craft, train up and give yourself the best chance possible.

I mean, can you imagine how many people casting directors see in one casting? Hundreds? Thousands? You need to do *whatever* you can to stand out.

When we submit for various roles, via breakdowns or through casting networks, for commercial or casting frontier and all those other platforms, they get a thumbnail; they get the notes we provide; and they get your reels. At some point, my bookers and I will go in and add notes to our talent because we make it our business to get to know who they are, and which roles we think are best for them to help them identify their niche.

As an actor, you think, "Oh, I can play anything and everything," but that's not necessarily true. Maybe what you have in your mind is the complete opposite of the kind of role that you're booking; sometimes that's just how it is. You have to see what the industry is saying and listen to that. People will book you if they know who you are and what you can do.

So, I know you have goals, where you want to be, and what you want to do. I'm not saying that you have to give up on those goals, but you've got to hone your niche and really bring that to the forefront.

Tone Capone

A&R and Development, Vice President of Motown Records, Music Industry

To me, it's just business. So, if I look at an artist, I'm looking at the overall picture. Is this person talented? Do they have the "X" factor? Do they light up a room? Do they light up a stage?

I remember The Fugees. When they first started out, they didn't have a hit record, but what made them stand out was the fact that they'd always have a great stage show. Their stage presence was incredible. They would come out there and get people thinking, *wow, you guys are great performers.* They may not have had a hit record, but they were good at their whole presentation, and their stage energy was incredible. So, when you left the event, you remembered them. You just paid more attention to them.

So, I would suggest making sure the whole package is presentable. I'm going to tell people, make sure you're ready. Don't waste an opportunity. A lot of people have it in their heads that they're already there and sometimes they're not. You need to be fully prepared. You need to be prepared to perform, prepared to deliver.

Artists come in for auditions for different labels and if they're not ready, then they'll fall flat and blow it. Once you blow your first chance, you're not coming back, at least not to that label, anyway.

Don't feel bad. Rejection is a part of success. You're going to go through a lot of rejection. It's like anything else. You need to be ready when walking in the door. If you're looking to take an exam and ace it first time, you have to study and you have to learn what's working and what's not. VIP Ignite gets you ready to ace the test.

You don't want to do the minimum to scrape by, and it's the same with your music. You need to test the marketplace, see what is happening, see if you're building some sort of buzz, and see if people have heard about you. You have to make sure that you meet the prerequisites.

So, to all these new artists: make sure you're ready. Make sure that you're confident enough that you can deliver. Don't blow your shot. If you want to come and deliver it, blow people away.

There is an artist that I discovered named Machine Gun Kelly. He goes by the name of MGK. He's an artist from Cleveland, Ohio. I was onstage hosting an event with around 800 people in the audience, and he stood up and yelled, "Hey, why don't you guys ever give us a shot? Why don't you guys ever give us an opportunity to show you what we're about?"

I had all the A&Rs, Anthony Rich from Jive Records, Lenny S. from Rockefeller, a whole bunch of them on stage with me. So, when this kid stood up and said that; I was like, "All right. Come on stage and show me what you got. I'll give you a shot." He was the one that stood up. He believed in himself. I was thinking, "All right. Show us what you got. Show us what you're about."

Then boom. He came onstage. He blew everybody away. And it all goes back to believing in yourself and having the confidence and delivering when you get the opportunity. If he would have come up and fallen flat on his face, he'd be nowhere today.

Here's the thing, though—you can't be so overconfident as to not have a plan. It's important that people plan and have a strategy. It can be as simple as I need to work on my music; I need to work on my stage presence; I need to make sure that when I get an opportunity, I'm able to deliver.

A lot of people don't plan and what happens? They fall short. So have a plan and keep the plan simple. Make sure your music sounds dope and make sure that you're 100% confident that you're ready to deliver.

I always tell people that your net worth equals your network. You've got to get out there, meet people, and shake hands. Be seen. Let people see you, and eventually, you'll connect with the right people in the right place at the right time.

Pat Addiss

Our Fairy Godmother, Jiminy Cricket, and Mary Poppins all in one, Broadway Producer and Broadway Expert

I think that you have to believe in yourself. Everybody has failures; rejection and failure are pretty much the same. You have to realize what the odds are, and you have to believe in yourself. I don't mean be arrogant, believing that you are the best, truly better than everybody else. I don't mean making the people around you nauseous from your over-indulgence in how great you are. What I mean is, believe that this is what you want to do and that you will succeed; believe that if you put the work in and keep going at it, you will do well.

This is a business and a lot of actors do not understand that this is a business. You've got to get up and do your act or whatever you're doing. If you're a playwright, you've got to get your work out there as much as you can. If you're a singer, then see if you can help do an open mic night or something at your local bar. If you're a dancer, put yourself out there and see if you can be a part of a local performance.

Do anything that you can do to get your name out there and get a credit. But that's the other thing, on your resume, don't lie.

Don't say that you were in such-and-such a show when you weren't because it is strange how small this industry really is. Somebody can pick up your resume and say, "Actually, no, you weren't in my show. Why did you put that on there?" Then suddenly your chances are gone.

However, there's a lot that you can put down that you don't even realize. Even if you're not getting paid for it but it is in the industry, you can put that down on your resume and also put down your special skills. Skills are very important, so if you speak Hungarian or Yiddish or whatever it is that you speak, that's a skill they should know about. If you do roller skating, that's a skill. Play an instrument, yeah, they want to hear about it. Put down any skill that you have, anything that can start building the bigger picture of you, because you never know what the little things can do for you.

Jam Murphy
Wilhelmina Model, Actress

When you focus on yourself, you attract the right people. I think that's important to say.

You've got to tap into what you need. You've got to look after your physical and mental health, first and foremost. I mean, keep your space clean, keep your body clean, keep your mind clean, and be mindful of what goes into your body, your mind, and your ears.

When you do that, then you can truly do the work, and not have to sit around waiting for somebody to call. There are ebbs and flows, but you have to keep going. There are slow times. You have to do something with that time.

One summer, I experienced one of those periods. Things were pretty slow, but I went out and learned to play golf. I went back to some old material and reworked it to keep it alive and I signed up for some different classes. You have to get through those periods, keep yourself busy, and not wait around. Keep yourself on a higher frequency, that way you'll be able to look after yourself.

I think this idea applies to anything, not just for working in the entertainment industry. If you treat your body right, then it's going to work better for you, and it's the same with your mental state. We have a very unstable schedule at times. This industry lacks structure.

I think you need to put your mental and physical health as a priority, especially when you get into acting. As an actor, you're doing all these difficult things and your body doesn't know that it's not real. You're taking on all these stresses, from action to tragedy, and your nervous system needs to be in check. Some people who work in this industry do it differently and are wonderful, but I think you'll have more longevity if you are healthier.

You gotta do the work. I've found that time and time again, if you don't feel like there's much going on, go back to the work and hone your craft; hone your instrument. Don't fall into the habit of reaching for somebody else or reaching for somebody to give you something. Don't wait, go inward, and do something to improve yourself.

Bill Walsh

CEO of PowerTeam International, America's Small Business Expert, Top Success Coach, Top Business Coach, Author

Success. I had the realization that I couldn't do it by myself. You can be good, but to really be great, become legendary or be a guru, it's not all about what you did to get it. It's about whether or not you served at a higher level and helped other people get what they wanted to get as well.

Once I learned to tap into that resource, where I would pour into people things that I could see, that they couldn't or even didn't want to see in themselves, that's when I found my success. I was brutally honest with it because there are enough programs out there to help you feel good. At the end of the day, when you're working at this level of any industry, I think people want you to give it to them straight. At the end of the day, people also need to hear the raw truth of what it takes to win.

The only way you can really understand this is through wisdom, and you can't buy wisdom. You receive it through experience; you receive it through failures, and you receive it through living life. It's funny that 20:20 vision is great, but hindsight, being able to go back and see forward, is 100 times more powerful than 20:20 vision. For me, I think it's forever a learning process and part of that is realizing that if you put yourself around the right people, magic will happen in your life.

Thomas G. Waites

Director, Producer, Writer

You can call it connections, you can call it networking, you can call it whatever you like, but the fact of the matter is, if people don't like you, they're not going to want to work with you. The people who work the most are the people who develop the best relationships with fellow actors, producers, writers, and directors because then those people want them back.

It's very simple. It's like a date. You don't go on a date with someone a second time if you know you don't like them. If they're negative, if they're uninteresting, if they're a sullen, sour, and solipsistic individual who lowers your frequency when you are around them, then they're not going to be a very pleasant date and you're probably not going to call them back.

So, when we talk about connections, what we're really talking about is the capacity to develop relationships. And much of that, at least in my case, comes from the fact that I grew up on a large island. You learned how to say please and thank you or you got whacked in the back of the head. You learned how to respect your sister, or she would punch you out, and you learned how to respect nature because your parents respected nature. So, when you went into the business world, you were familiar with how to interact with other people on a deeply interpersonal level. The key to that, as I'm sure you know and if you don't then you soon will, is finding out about other people.

If you're interviewing with a director, a producer or casting director and there's a picture of their kid on the desk, ask about that. Or if they have a photo from a holiday or of a pet, ask about it. People love to be asked questions about themselves. It makes them feel important, but I think that it's also a kind of common courtesy, isn't it?

The more specific you can be in your questioning, the more you can learn and connect with that person. Obviously, you don't want to be asking questions like, "What's your bra size?" because that is crossing boundaries. But be curious. Ask where they're from, for example, then ask whereabouts in that country, county, or city they're from because you never know where a connection could arise. You might have lived in similar areas or even worked in that city and immediately you have a connection. If you know something about them, you understand them better.

So, try to find those connections because what you really want to do is build relationships from them.

Vincent Rodriguez III
Actor, Voice-Actor, Broadway Actor, Singer, Dancer, Teacher, Mentor

If I were to encapsulate everything and translate it into a piece of advice that you could use to help you in whatever it is you are doing, I would say, take the time to be aware of yourself and the things around you. This is straight out of an Amanda Owen book, *The Power of Receiving*, but open your hands up and welcome all the things you're afraid of. Welcome all those things you want to avoid simply because you don't want to deal with them for whatever reason; welcome those things that you've put off, that you've diverted from, and that you've pushed away.

This is a new concept for me, and you're probably wondering why I would do any of that. Well, when you welcome all those things, you're in "receiving" mode. Imagine your hands out, ready to receive something, and you will get more when you are in this mode.

Yes, it's uncomfortable, but being uncomfortable is a part of your human existence.

We are not done. In order to grow, to excel, to make everything we have, we had to do something called failing. From failure, we can grow and create more abundance. When we step out of our comfort zone, we can think outside the box and innovate and collaborate. Uncomfortable is necessary.

So, for those of you who are uncomfortable, who are going through discomfort, and who feel that it's too much, I totally understand where you're at. I know where you're coming from. And the best piece of loving and caring advice I can give you is to create a relationship with that discomfort by just sitting with it.

I know it sounds crazy. Actually, sit with it. Write down how you feel. Find an outlet for all those emotions and express them. I'm not saying take it out on someone that you love, I'm saying express it.

Maybe you're a dancer. Maybe you're a painter. Maybe you're a musician. Maybe you love axe throwing. Maybe you love bowling. Or maybe you love baking.

Whatever your art is, because art is everywhere and in everything we do, find your outlet, because life is all about balance. It's a balance of the dark and the light, of the pros and the cons, of those awesome moments that we love. We live for those pros, but we also live for everything in between.

I know what it feels like to be in the state of being overwhelmed, where you feel like you can't handle it, that it's all too much. But remember, you are stronger than you think. Until you face those things that you're afraid of, you won't get to know that with certainty or confidence.

Have a relationship with whatever "it" is. Face those fears and that discomfort. Sit there and realize it's not that bad. Or realize it does suck and is just as horrible as you thought it was. You now know how to cope with it and you're okay with it—even if it is horrible. It's kind of like finally meeting that dog in the neighborhood that is never on a leash; you're no longer scared of it because you know it.

I've done that. I've made a lot of different choices in the last eight months, and it was super uncomfortable. It was the quintessential definition of discomfort. I felt icky, felt my body temperature rise, and it was gross. I remember thinking to myself that this is actually what it takes to be at the artistic standard that I want to maintain and continue to progress in the areas I want to excel in. It took me a long time to find that for myself. When I found that, it made it a lot easier to say no to certain things, whether it be a job or a party.

This industry has a lot of opportunities, and you could say yes to everything, but you need to be careful when you do say yes because when you say yes, you also say no to so many other things. I read somewhere that when you say no to something once, you say yes to yourself twice.

When you say no, you are staying aligned with your goals. You have a vision of your career, of where you want to go, and what kind of person you want to be. When you say no to a project, you're saying no because it's not in line with what you want to be doing. The second yes you give yourself is in confidence. You're saying that you believe in yourself and in where you're going.

In this industry, you will hear a lot of people say, "Oh, but I need the job." No, you don't. You might need *a* job, but you don't always need *that* job. There are a lot of jobs out there, so you can always find the one that is right for you. It's not going to be easy, but things don't get easy, you just get better.

Now, to a lot of people, I know this may sound a little too intense. I've gotten that a lot but it's part of who I am, and it's gotten me results. However, I did it for a long time with a perfectionist mindset and that actually ruined me.

I had to learn to give up the things that were in my way. I gave up the perfectionism and the worrying, and I gave up listening to the two imposters: Applause and Rejection.

I replaced perfectionism with curiosity. I replaced worrying and thinking about the uncertain future, with excitement, anticipation, and gratitude for what the future could be. Instead of paying attention to the applause, the likes, the awards and the rejections, the judgments, or the critics, I've started to pay attention to myself. I replaced them both with self-love. I believe 100% in the idea that nothing anyone says is going to stop me from doing what I love and what I wake up every morning motivated and inspired to do.

So, if you know that, even if you don't know what you're inspired to do yet, you know that there is a future version of yourself who loves you entirely. That version loves what you're doing, loves who you're around, loves how you live, and loves who you have become. When you have that knowledge and certainty, then there's balance and your life can be way more fulfilling.

CHAPTER 5

IGNITING THE PASSION

The biggest thing is perseverance, passion, patience, and persistence – the four Ps.

Whether you're in front of the camera or behind the camera,

you need perseverance, persistence, patience, and passion.

If you have those, you will do well in the business.

You may not become Julia Roberts or Leonardo DiCaprio,

but you will work and you will do well in the business.

– *Roxanne Messina Captor*

VIP IGNITE IS THE SECOND SECRET TO YOUR SUCCESS.

The first is a combination of the right mindset and skill set. Some would say that one is easier to obtain than the other, as you can work on getting the right skills to succeed, but having the right mindset is almost like having the "it" factor. Here's something to start with—a way to get you into the right mindset:

- What is your purpose for being in this industry?

- What is the one thing you can focus on?

For example, if you're trying to find a white-label company to promote your makeup line, you need to be able to focus on one thing that's not going to get you running around in circles chasing your tail. Rather than trying to focus on the end goal or the bigger picture, focus on a singular outcome that will support what you ultimately want to achieve as your end goal. It could be designing the right branding, finding the right slogan, or organizing promotional material for a folio.

Whatever it is, by just focusing on one little thing, you can suddenly make the impossible possible. When you complete that thing, check it off, and file it away. You know that you're free to move on to the next step. This was my first step to success, changing my mindset and becoming more focused on what I needed to do and what I needed to know in order to get to where I wanted to be.

When you talk business with people, they have millions of ideas going and they're just running in circles. So many of them try to chase everything at once. They spread themselves too thin and don't put 100% of themselves into any one thing. It was something I used to do. I would try to juggle twenty different things and was almost always surprised when I couldn't keep it up. Some people thrive on being able to juggle as much as they can, but for most of us, it's better to focus on one thing at a time. It's how you can get the ball rolling.

This is just one thing though, right? A small change can

make all the difference to how successful you can become, but there is also something else that ensures you have the right mindset for not only surviving but truly thriving in this industry. It's something that cannot be taught, no matter how hard you try. *It's not only perseverance and persistence, it's passion.*

DETERMINATION TO STAND OUT

Can you name the actors in your favorite TV show without looking them up? Or do you just know them by their characters? Is the only reason you know who they are because they're big names in the industry? These people are getting paid $65,000 an episode. They've worked their whole lives to build their career, to be the co-star or star of a show, but most people don't even know their acting name.

That's 99% of the industry. People see a familiar face and go, "Oh, I know that guy! What's his name? Oh, you know, he was the guy on Boardwalk Empire. He was on the Sopranos, remember?" Outside of the twelve or thirteen actors that people recognize, most people won't know the acting name of most of the stars. Take the lead for the show *Billions*. He's the star of one of the biggest shows on TV right now, but if I were to ask you his name, you'd likely have no idea.

Or take another example, who plays the villain in *Breaking Bad*? Don't know? His name is Giancarlo Esposito. He played Akela in Disney's *The Jungle Book* and, more recently, portrays Moff Gideon in *the Mandalorian* series. He's a fantastic actor and yet most people don't know his name. Even looking at someone more prolific from the show, do you know what Jesse

Pinkman's acting name is? I can bet that even if you watched every season, there's still a chance you don't know his acting name.

You know the show. You know the characters. You're invested in their stories but didn't take the time to learn who is playing the character. That is, unless they're making headlines consistently. But a lot of the younger generation won't even know that. Instead, they know the names of TikTok and YouTube celebrities. Those people have huge followings. They are social media influencers. Even if they only have a couple dozen followers, there's a bigger chance that young people will know their name. They know the names of these people over famous actors because that's who they're exposing themselves to. It's constant and consistent.

Mr. Beast has one of the most watched channels on YouTube, with one of the highest subscriber counts as of this year. He brings in more than $100 million a year and he gives away most of that money every single day. He does videos where he'll go to a restaurant, order a cheeseburger, then leave the waitresses $200,000 tips. He'll go into a grocery store, and he'll pay for the groceries for the entire grocery store. Mr. Beast makes a big impact, and it shows in his following, but I bet Tony Robbins probably wouldn't even know who he is. It shows you how hard it is to break through in this industry; to become a household name. There is a good chance that everyday people won't ever know your name. It takes an enormous amount of time and effort to make that impact enough for people to actually recognize your face and name. Making enough of an impact is exhausting, and it doesn't happen to everyone. Sometimes it never happens, because not everyone can have that constant consistency. To get that, you have to be pushed into the spotlight all the time. You have to be on the front page of the papers or appear on people's newsfeeds every time they open their phones. You have to get yourself out there at a level that it becomes impossible for people not to know who you are.

Even models and musicians go through the same thing, people know their faces and know the music, but they don't know who *they* are. The point is, these people still get work, right? It's because these people stand out to the right people. They have the drive and passion to stand out in the industry so that the right people know their names.

Years ago, I was talking to one of the groups of casting directors who, at that time, handled the Marvel castings in New York City. They had come to one of our events and commented on the quality of the talent we had there. They asked for my secret and were quite persistent about it. They wanted to know how a few hundred of our models, actors, musicians, and other talents all had the spark that they only ever saw in maybe ten or twenty of the thousands who would come to their auditions. I had to disappoint them and tell them there wasn't a secret to creating the spark. We only fostered the fire they already had.

We put a lot of time into working with the talent who join us. We make sure they know what to do and understand each aspect of the world they want to be a part of, but the thing we *don't* give them is their fire. We help to ignite that fire, but all the talent who come to VIP Ignite have an energy that cannot be taught. They all have that spark because they want this more than life itself. They want to make it happen and will navigate every road they can to achieve the dream. Sometimes it's the experience that closes the deal but having that fire can really set you apart from the crowd.

Think about it. If you're a model, actor, or even a musician, what sets you apart from all the other people in the room bidding for the same opportunity? If you don't have that enthusiasm, that fire, why would directors or producers want to hire you?

You want to stand out. Personality and attitude can make or break you when it comes to first impressions. I remember one time I was doing an audition with the Vice President of Warner Brothers. It was casting for one of the early seasons of *Survivor* and there were about 800 guys there waiting in line, but they only needed one. It was a stressful job, both for those auditioning and for the one filtering through the talent, but I will always remember what he said to me when I brought up the notion of stress. He said, you can either be stressed out trying to find the one, or you can spend the day getting rid of 799.

The reason I think this has stayed with me is that it shows just how much of an impact you need to have on a casting director when you walk into that room. That day when we came up to the building, there were already people outside smoking. There were a couple of folks arguing over the phone; some people hadn't even turned up; then there was one guy who didn't have a care in the world as he slept on the floor and blocked the corridor. What we saw before the audition even started was incredible. The faces of the people who didn't have the right attitude while waiting for the audition were the ones you would recognize when they walked into the room.

You want to have the right mindset both in and out of the audition room because, like your social media, you never know what people might see. You want to make sure they're getting the best impression of you from the outset.

GETTING MORE THAN YOUR FOOT IN THE DOOR

So, let's say you have the passion and you come to us with an open mind, ready to change your outlook on your approach to success. What then?

Do you wait around in the hopes that your big break will find you, or do you stay persistent and persevere with each and every little thing that brings you one step closer to the dream?

Well, if you've been following me on my journey as you're starting on yours, you'll know that the first option isn't even an option. That big break doesn't just happen, even if you have the right mindset. As you get your foot on the first rung of the ladder and you begin that climb, you have to be ready to take on just about any job.

Actors can't expect speaking parts at the beginning of their careers. Models can't expect to be on magazine covers when they've only done a few small photoshoots. And aspiring musicians might have to accept being backup for a while. You have to be ready to do a lot of hard work for not much money or fame. It can be discouraging and difficult to remain positive when you do so much and get so little in return, but in this industry, experience is everything and everyone wants experience. It's why the events and boot camps that we host try to accelerate the experience of our talent, giving them exposure to all areas of the entertainment industry as well as the connections they need to get a head start. It's why those who work with us hold on to that spark and stay inspired.

A lot of people, when they get over that hurdle and get

their foot in the door, start to worry about all the "what-ifs." For example, a lot of aspiring actors worry about being typecast before they've even walked into the audition, and for others, it's worrying about when is the right time to move to L.A. or New York before they've really made a name for themselves where they are at that moment. We try to help our talent understand the process and give them the knowledge and skills to navigate the industry.

Another thing we try to do is move them away from having a mindset where they fixate on the what-ifs and instead develop what we call a growth mindset. You want to grow and learn as much as you can. Take all the opportunities you can. And seeing each one in a positive light. You have to have a can-do mindset and be able to stay focused rather than constantly thinking about what you can't do and overwhelming yourself with the bigger picture.

Many of our beginner training sessions and events are designed to instil this ideology to help our talent overcome negative language and thought patterns. So many people have been told to not even try because it's too hard and they get stuck in that mindset. They have the idea cemented in their heads that they can't do it for one reason or another. They'll say they don't have the money, or the time, or the skill, or even more simply, for whatever reason, they just can't.

That is the mentality we encourage our talent to move away from. We want them to have confidence in themselves and their ability. When they can change that narrative and language for themselves, they can use that ability to change the tonality of monologues and scripts. Everything starts to work for them, and rather than being generalized, each experience is individualized. I think this has a lot to do with why our talent becomes so much more successful so much faster than those who are just attending sessions or lessons with teachers.

At the start of your career, you need to be making smart decisions, looking ahead, and making sure you're not getting stuck at the bottom. You can do it on your own, but it's easier to do it with someone to guide you.

I live my life working with models, actors, and musicians, but I've also spent a lot of time working with casting directors, and producers, and even invested thousands of dollars in Broadway productions. It's given me the ability to see the industry from various perspectives, from the good and the bad.

I want to make it clear that I have no problem with people going out to pay for an education. What I have a problem with, is when the people doing the educating are not properly educated themselves. Some "schools" have a textbook training program where they teach you how to do your hair, how to have poise, how to do your nails, or look good for the camera. They sell it as "How to Become a Model" but it's really just a "charm school." It's a really expensive charm school where the people teaching the classes have no real experience in the industry and maybe only graduated a month prior.

Even outside of institutions offering an education, I've seen so many different people offering help to those looking to start their journey in the entertainment industry. Those people give a little bit of advice on what they know and offer a few nuggets that might be helpful in certain circumstances. But it's because of those certain circumstances that they're not helping people. These people are often actors who have never gotten their big break, musicians who have never gotten a hit song, or models who never made it onto the runway.

They're people who have never gotten to the end of the road and instead turned their efforts to coaching new talent.

At the end of the day, a lot of these people have the wrong mindset when it comes to the industry and end up creating that same mindset in the newcomers they advise. They know how to attend auditions, write songs, and pose for photographs. They've probably been in front of numerous casting directors and producers and just never gotten lucky.

To these people, the industry has become very black-and-white. They believe there has to be a villain in the story, so to the talent, it's the producers and directors; whereas, for the producers and directors, it's the aspiring talent that sends them a demo or walks into the audition room. They don't understand what it's like to look at the industry from a different perspective.

For example, a person trained as an actor only knows to look at things from the perspective of an actor, just as most casting directors or producers only know how to see things from the perspective of their positions. If you end up getting caught up in the views of one person who failed, you're not going to get the best perspective, and when those voices leave you, you will be suddenly lost with nowhere to go.

What we at VIP Ignite try to do is to educate those who come to our events and help them understand the industry. We teach them that even though advice can be helpful, it can also end up being costly, especially if you're following models that didn't work for the people doing the coaching. Avoiding that type of advice is an easy way to avoid a lot of confusion as well.

I don't care how small a market there is where you are. You can start building your resume and you can start earning money. You don't need to be in Hollywood; you don't need to be in New York. You might want that to be your destination, but sometimes, thinking small and simple is the best start you can have. Stepping away from the bigger picture, breaking things down, and focusing on those little things sets you on your journey.

Find out everything that is going on in your community, anywhere there could be work. It's possible that someone has already created or advertised possibilities. There's so much in your local area that you could take advantage of. It might only be a few adverts or photoshoots, a background role in the seasonal show, but every little thing that you can do before you take that leap into the wider world of the entertainment industry is invaluable. Most people who are looking to find their footing in this industry often underestimate the value of what is going on nearby. Instead, they turn their attention to the online space, but one of the worst places you can go to start looking for work is the internet.

There was a girl from Montana who came to us after she had spent tens of thousands of dollars on training and classes, doing everything she could to propel herself toward that big break. But it never really happened. She came to us as very much a big fish in a small pond who hadn't looked at what was in that small pond.

I remember talking to her and asking if she had looked at what was on her doorstep, asking if she had gone to the Montana Film Board. I was surprised when she said no. She was aiming so high that she was discouraging and disempowering herself. She was getting into that negative mindset of believing she wasn't going to get anywhere when she simply wasn't looking in the right places.

So, I pulled up the casting opportunities for Montana. I remember there were two at the time; she applied to one, and she got it. She became an actress in Montana and now she's part of the Montana Film Board. It was the simplest thing, and it changed her life, but it's not the thing that most people think of when they think of this industry.

People spend all their money with Hollywood in mind. But you're never really going to start in Hollywood unless you already live there. Moving to Hollywood or New York, the epicenters of the entertainment industry, should always be a part of the destination. It should never be at the start of your journey. Instead, change your perspective and, with it, your mindset. Sometimes thinking small and thinking simple can be easier than expected. You just have to persevere, stay persistent and ignite your passions in all you do.

INTERVIEWS FROM THE INDUSTRY, PART FOUR

Les Brown
Motivational Speaker, Politician, Former Ohio State Representative

Nietzsche said, "If you know the why, you can live anyhow."

When I decided I wanted to be a speaker, I knew that the reason I wanted to do that was to be able to make a difference in people's lives. But I also wanted to be able to be in a position to take care of my mother, so that if something were ever to happen as she got older, she could call on me and I would be able to be there for her. Those reasons made me unstoppable and hungry to face all the rejections and all the setbacks. I ignored all the naysayers and did not stop until I was able to establish a level of mastery so good at what I did that I could not be ignored.

We all have that greatness. It's inborn and inside all of us. But persistence is what makes the difference between those who make it and those who don't.

In the beginning, I had no connections, but my hunger and the impact that I could make on the lives of the people I spoke to, allowed me to break through and draw attention to myself. That persistence, the hunger, was what allowed me to start making those connections.

I wanted to become a disc jockey and when I first went to Milton Butterball Smith, the then program director at WMBM Radio Station, he said no. I had no experience, no journalism experience, no broadcasting background, nothing, so I went away and I told my mentor, Mr. Leroy Washington. He said, "If you want to make it, you gotta be hungry." He told me to go back because you have to fail on your way to success.

So, I went back and I said, "Hello Mr. Butterball. My name is Les Brown, and, sir, I'd like to be a disc jockey." And he replied, "Didn't I tell you no yesterday?" I said, "Yes sir, but I don't know if somebody was laid off or somebody was fired." He then said, "No one was laid off or fired. Now get on out of here." I left, and then I came back the next day, and the next day, and the next day. Every day, I said, "Hello Mr. Butterball, how are you? My name is Les Brown, and, sir, I'd like to be a disc jockey," until the day came, when after saying, "Hello," he replied, "I know who you are, now go get me some coffee."

I got my foot in the door, and I would have done anything and everything for them. I wanted to position myself in their minds as a resourceful person. I would get their lunch, drive them around, and all the while, I memorized the controls because it's better to be prepared for an opportunity and not have one than to have an opportunity and not be ready for it.

One day, a disc jockey named Rockin Rodger was drinking while he was on the air and was slurring his words. It was obvious he could not complete the show. I was the only other one there and I knew the general manager was listening, as he always did, so when the phone rang, I picked it up. When he said, "Hello young man, this is Mr. Klein." I replied, "I know." He wanted one of the other DJs to come in and finish the show, and I knew this was my opportunity. So, I called him back and said there was nobody. He asked if I knew how to work the drill and I said yes. He told me to go on there and work it, but to say nothing. But I also knew it was easier to be forgiven than to ask for permission.

There is a song called *Fingertips*, written by Stevie Wonder when he was twelve years old. I opened with that song and said, "Look out, this is me, LB Triple P, Les Brown, your platter plan papa. There were none before me and there will be none after me, and therefore that makes me the one and only. I'm young and single, love to mingle, certified, bona fide, and duly qualified to bring you satisfaction with a whole lot of action. Look out baby, I'm your love man!"

I was hungry, and ol' Rock was lying there on the floor. I was hungry, and I took the opportunity. I even got the job there shortly after, but it was that hunger that got me through.

I heard something once; it's simple, but it's real. Nothing is as powerful as persistence. The world is full of unsuccessful people with talent. Genius alone will not make it; unrewarded genius is almost a proverb. Education alone will not make it; the world is full of educated derelicts. *Persistence and determination alone are omnipotent.*

Even a broken clock is right twice a day. If you keep striking, something will break hard!

Scott Patrick Erwin

Actor, Model, Writer

Any advice that I would give is that you have to be the one to decide where you want to go with this. Be very realistic but do everything you can within you to keep going in that direction, commit 100%, and do what is required to get where you want to be. Make the choice and get whatever help you need to get there. Get an education, get the training, and whatever discipline you need to continue, just go and improve those skills.

We've only got one life.

People say it flippantly, but we really do only have one. So, if there is something you want to do, make the choice and do it. If you want to be a part of this industry, then it's not going to look like everybody else's life, and you have to make peace with that.

My friends are not going to auditions. My friends are not going to photoshoots. The people in my life, who are not a part of this industry, are not doing what I am doing. Most of them can't imagine doing something like this in midlife like me.

They don't always understand, and you have to be able to stand your ground. They may try to be supportive, but they are not going to really understand how to be supportive. Sometimes they think they do, but they don't. They will try to offer what they think is helpful, but what they're doing is trying to break you down. So, you have to be able to push through that, even when it's coming from a really "influential" place.

I come from a professional background. I'm a CPA, I have an MBA, I've been a CFO, and worked for large, multinational companies. When I told my father that I was going to leave all that behind and pursue a creative career in acting and writing, he said to me, in frustration, "So you know you have to admit that this isn't going to happen for you." I remember turning to him, and saying, "No, I don't have to admit that." And he thought he was being helpful by asking, "Well, how long are you going to do this for?"

I am going to do this until the day I die. I had made that choice. This is what I want to do, but he just couldn't grasp that in his mind. He's "supportive" but from his perspective. I have had to make peace with that and forgive him for not understanding. I had to learn to let those kinds of comments slide off. It's challenging and it's not easy, especially when it's family. That's still something that is really, really difficult to overcome.

When I first got into VIP Ignite, I heard some of the coaches, teachers, mentors, and other actors say that if you have any doubts about this life, if you can do any better and feel fulfilled in that, go do it because this is not an easy life. There may be prizes and the glamour that may come with it eventually, but the point is that's *eventually*.

I'll use an analogy from *Rocky*. When you see Rocky in the ring, you think, "Oh, this is great!" But you kind of forget that 80% of the movie was watching him training. It was seeing him fail, get hurt, and be discouraged. The real message in that story is seeing his ability to get back up and keep going.

In all practical purposes, that's what a career in the creative industry is like. You have to keep creating and hoping that something works and that you're going to get somewhere with it. As they say, the harder you work, the luckier you get, but you have to figure out how to work hard and still be joyful about going in this direction—even when it gets difficult.

Jeffrey Gurian
Actor, Comedian, Writer, Producer

It took me many years to get out on stage and perform. I was writing for a lot of big stars before I started performing, but I had another problem because I used to be a cosmetic dentist. While I was in my dental practice, I was also writing for Rodney Dangerfield and Joan Rivers, so it made it very complicated because I was combining two careers. It was a gradual transition to full-time writing because I did both for many years.

I was writing for the Friars' Club, and I wrote for some of the greats, like Milton Berle and Jerry Lewis. Milton Berle was my sponsor in the Friars' Club. I would be in my office, calls would come in, and my nurse had strict instructions to never disturb me unless it was show business. She would come in and say, Dr. Berle or Dr. Lewis is on the phone. The only one nobody would ever believe was Dr. Dangerfield. There couldn't be a Dr. Dangerfield.

I was doing both and making it work, but you know the idea is to start young and persevere because it's very difficult to break in. It's not like it was years ago, when you could go to clubs and meet people. That's what I used to do. It's not as easy anymore, but you can do it. You should start hanging out at the comedy clubs, to let people see you, to become known, and very politely introduce yourself to somebody that you like.

Most of the comedians are very approachable, not all of them, but most of them are. Some don't talk to people, but that's a whole other story.

I used to go up to the Catskills a lot when the Catskills were still a big draw and the big comedy stars would be performing in the hotels. It was easier then. I would wait for them after the show, and I would introduce myself and tell them I was a comedy writer. I asked them if they would allow me to try to write some material for them.

And here's the thing, if you speak well and you present yourself well, then there's a good chance that someone will give you a shot. You're not asking them for any investment, and most people will take that chance if you give them the right impression.

But you have to go and see who you feel you could write for. I'm gearing this toward comedians, but this pertains to any entertainer. Start young and persevere because most of the time you get turned down in show business. It's a very difficult thing and you need to build up a little bit of a thick skin; you must believe in yourself if you think that you're funny or talented or beautiful and you want to model, play a musical instrument, whatever. If *you* think that you're good, then you have to persevere no matter what anybody says to you, because if you don't do that, it'll torture you for your whole life.

Michael Stonewall Beaudry
Casting Director

I was an English major in college. I actually have degrees in English and history, and I worked on a novel out of college because I wanted to write. I love telling stories and I love being part of the process.

When I came here, I worked as a Director of Development for production companies. I worked in international sales and domestic distribution for a boutique film company that did pretty well for itself. We had an Oscar-nominated film five years in a row for Best Documentary and/or Best Foreign Language Film. I really wanted to get into writing, but I needed a job.

I asked a friend if I could work in casting, and he said he would help me out. So, he introduced me to a few casting directors. I got the sense they liked me, and they did because, well, they hired me. People might like you and want to hire you immediately, but that doesn't mean they have a job for you. It's not a nine-to-five, Monday through Friday job.

As a casting director, you will get three jobs a week and then you won't work for a month. So, you have to wait until they need someone and hopefully, when they do, they'll remember you.

You have to have the availability to work when they need you *if* they need you. You have to wait and wait and wait, hoping that you're the one they want to use. Once you get used, then you'll get used again and again and you'll love it.

When you don't get hired for weeks, it can feel like you did something wrong, but it's usually nothing against you. It's usually that the person who has been with them longer was available again.

When you start working as a casting director, it's good to be working at studios that have multiple offices of casting directors because that way you can put your eggs in a million different baskets. That was the advice my friend gave me.

If you put all your eggs in one basket, other casting

directors will find it hard to hire you and when the one gets slow, you won't have work. And there's not much you can do about it because they have total control over you.

I worked in a number of places, and it took a while before I got my first job. But for that job, I did a bunch more all because they liked and remembered me. I loved it and the rest is kind of history.

It's fun and fast-paced, and you get to work with some of the greatest visual artists of our time, and frankly some of the greatest musical artists of all time. When you get there, it makes it all worthwhile. It's such an unbelievable privilege and honor when people are trusting you to help craft the look, the feel, the energy, and the very heart of their project.

Sometimes you can look at a finished project and just see your work all over it and then other times, you can feel like you didn't do anything at all. That's okay. Sometimes you're just there to provide due diligence and that's okay too. For me, it was an ego blow at first; it was confusing, but eventually, it didn't really matter. It's just a project. If the filmmakers are happy, if the directors are happy, if everyone's pleased, and all you did was help and advise, then that's enough.

Roxanne Messina Captor
Director, Producer, Writer

I think it doesn't hurt to try to put yourself out there, but if you get a no, then you get a no. There are always times you can try to turn things around, but the truth is that, for most people who are on the executive side, their job is to say no; their job isn't to say yes. You have to say, "I *really* want to do this," and go for it, and then learn from the mistakes. Find that fine line between being aggressive and not being so pushy that people get angry with you.

What I do sounds great on paper, but there was also all the downtime that no one talks about. There was the downtime when I got those no's and when I didn't have work, so I was strictly teaching or doing crazy little things. I don't know how many times I did product demonstrations in stores for various companies like Kodak cameras, Royal Copenhagen, and Lauren perfume, but I did all those things because you've got to keep working while you're trying to get jobs.

There are times when you think, *Should I get out? Is this worth it?* You have to have that underlying, driving passion that says, "Well, this is who I am, this is what I am about, and this is what I know. I'm here, and I have something to offer." Sometimes it's hard, but it keeps you going.

You'll have downtime and you may stop for a while, but as long as you're persistent, then you will find work. I got asked to choreograph a show at a regional theater outside of New York, and I remember going to lunch with the producer. We had a very "adult" conversation about the show, and he was interested in my ideas, so we talked about money. I consider myself to be a very good negotiator, so I got what I was asking for.

After that, I was offered to do a lot of shows. A regional theater asked me to do a performance in Chicago and there was another one that was doing a national tour, but I just really didn't have any interest in performing. Accepting them would have meant going into intense, solid training for six months or more, and I was not there for it. Now, I take dance classes for my own enjoyment, or I do Pilates or yoga, but it's all for my own health and enjoyment. I don't have to prove anything.

I did some choreography, and then some of the theaters I choreographed allowed me to direct and choreograph some musicals. I continued doing that out here on the West Coast. I've done musicals and plays up and down the coast, because I love theater, but I never thought of myself as being in film or TV. It just sort of happened. I got the opportunity to work with Gene Kelly, which led to getting to know Francis Ford Coppola, which then led to so much other stuff.

What I found, at least in my career, is you keep pounding and pounding and pounding, and it seems like everything you're pounding on never comes to fruition, but then all of a sudden, something else comes from a whole other direction. An opportunity just comes in a completely different way, and you think, "Where did that come from?" It's where you're meant to be, and sometimes that's just what happens.

These things come to you in very odd, weird ways, but only because you've kept working or kept pounding away. Maybe the thing you're pounding on doesn't yield any opportunities right away, or even ever, but because you did that, it opens other doors. You worked really hard; you went to all the auditions, you networked, and you did all that stuff, and something happened because of it.

Robert Russell
VP of Warner Brothers Casting (retired)

Personality overrides everything else, and in an audition, you have two- or three-minutes tops. Your job as an actor is to go in there and blow us away, not only with your talent but with your personality. We have to love you as soon as you walk into the room. Before you even open your mouth, we have to love you. You make us love you by your attitude and presence; that's what it means to have a big personality. You can't come in shy or fumbling your words or cowering away from the table; you have to come in already presenting that big personality.

I have met some actors along the way, in my journey, with astonishing personalities, and I know actors that have booked auditions and feature films, just based on personality alone. So, that absolutely overrides everything. There is no way you can come in half-cocked. Casting directors know you. We know you before you even open your mouth. It's like a sixth sense that we have. We know this; we've been doing this forever; we know you as soon as you walk into the room. We see your body language and that's what we look for. After you get past that, it's time to shine. Now you have to show us what you can do.

Acting is an art.

It's like being a classically trained ballet dancer—you're not just dancing; you're creating an experience full of emotion and connection. As an actor, you're not just taking lines off a page; you want to create that same experience every time you audition.

I have an actor who's been training since she was fourteen. I brought her in to see an agent because she was ready for a feature film. She was the kind of girl where the stars would one day align, and she would be the next big thing. She was gonna be thrust into that machine, and you know what? She was ready like you have no idea; her tools are polished and honed, and she's completely crafted. That's what we want to see.

A headshot and resume are a picture and words on a page to me, what matters is what you do in front of me. I want to see how crafted an actor is, and crafted means trained.

It's like training for a championship fight. All the heavyweight greats weren't sitting at a bar getting fat, they were in the gym training to be the best because that's ultimately what they wanted to do; they wanted to get to the end of the road and win that championship belt. It's the same thing with an actor, you've got to go after it like that.

All professional actors are fully trained, they're all trained method actors because when they were coming up and they were auditioning and had no money, that's what they were doing. They had great acting coaches and dialect coaches; they were spending every little dime they had to get some good training with good people.

I give movies to my actors to watch, and I insist that they know every actor in the movie and their body of work, every director, everything, so they know what they're talking about. You need to be so well-rounded in this business and prepared that there's nothing you don't know as an actor. All of that builds your confidence and allows you to walk into that room with no fear and take over. That's your job as an actor: to walk in and take over and splatter our guts all over the wall.

Patrick Quagliano

Head of Stella Alder, Acting Coach of the Stars

An actor who has had training sees differently; they understand what it takes to play a character and they can look outside of themselves. They have a developed imagination; they know how to experience and see the world of the play from different points of view. There is a magic about them; there is curiosity; there is maturity; there is confidence. It is so different when you're trained.

You may laugh, but if you go to a doctor and he has no training, how long will it take you to see that? Well, it is the same with an actor. I can tell when they've opened their eyes. I can tell when they walk into a room. An actor who is trained doesn't go right to the words; something happens before they even open their mouth. There is no fear, no fear. When they open their eyes, they see something. They take themselves somewhere else and you suddenly go with them. With technology and how fast the world is moving nowadays, everybody wants things yesterday. But guess what? Acting training is not instant coffee. It's not something you just brew up.

I am competing against a world where everybody wants success and results now. That's what technology has done, and I work against that all the time. The instrument has to be nurtured. It has to be developed and it has to be given time to grow. It doesn't all happen all presto.

Ideally, actors should train for two to three years, but I will tell you, the best is four years: two years of training and then two years of doing productions. Have experience with productions before you go out there and get paid for it. More and more people are doing that now. If you are one of those who just want to go out to L.A. after five weeks of training and try it out, well, good luck to you, but you're not going to have a career if you do it that way.

Marthe Reynolds
VP Island – Def Jam (retired)

If someone comes to me and says, I really want to sing. Well, okay, I can't make you an artist: you have to already be an artist and then come to me. You have to come to me fully formed; you have to come to me as an artist. I am the facilitator; you are the artist. I can't throw pixie dust on you and make people love you. I need to hear music that is ready. Even if you're a DJ, I need to feel your sweat and your DNA in the work that I am listening to, the equity. When everybody else is out partying and getting high, you are in the studio. I want somebody who is committed to being an artist.

It is a bumpy road, and it is not a sprint, it really is a marathon, as they say. If I listen and hear you off-key, off-pitch, or auto-tuning all over the record, I just can't listen anymore, because there are people out there who can actually sing and perform. I think I am doing them a disservice by taking time to listen to your weakly produced, weakly constructed project.

If you send me something that is misspelled or the grammar is incorrect, you need to get some help presenting it. If you give me a bio that is full of grammatical errors and misspellings, I will not read it. It's all about presentation, and if you didn't care enough to fix it, then I don't care enough to review it. You need to work on it, because, if *you* don't care, *I* don't care.

CHAPTER 6

IGNITING THE TALENT

You know the old joke about how do you get to Carnegie Hall?

Practice, practice, practice.

You have to be skilled in your craft.

You can't just go in there and not be prepared,

so if you're auditioning for something,

get as much preparation as possible.

If you're doing La Cage aux Folles, listen to the recording.

If there's a video, watch the video.

Learn the part that you're auditioning for.

Be as prepared as you possibly can be.

– Pat Addiss

If you want to have the right opportunities and meet the right people, you have to have the determination to go out and find them. When the moment comes and you find yourself in the right place at the right time, you only have one chance to make that first impression.

I truly feel the more you can learn on your own, and the more skills you can master, the more potential there is to compensate for a lack of experience. When you go to an audition, you might not have the same level of experience as some of the other people auditioning, but if you've been able to accumulate a collection of skills that they don't have, you suddenly stand out. Perhaps you've had that chance to take some training with the senior stunt coordinator who worked with the cast of *The Walking Dead*, or perhaps you've been able to work with 50 Cent's acting coach, or even had the opportunity to have theater training with Ben Crawford.

Having a chance to learn skills this way, let alone having the opportunity to associate yourself with these kinds of people, isn't as impossible as it might seem. VIP Ignite was created to make these opportunities possible. We invite people to our events so that our guests and talents can have the chance to build connections and possibly the chance to improve their skills.

When it comes to building skills and connections in your journey to discovering opportunity, persistence, perseverance, and passion are key. There's a great example of this in an old-school story of a young guy who brought a headshot every single day to every single agency and casting director he could. Every day he was faced with rejection and after about a month one of the girls at an agency's front desk told him straight up that she threw his headshots in the garbage, that the agency and directors weren't interested in him, and they likely never would be. So, from then on alongside his headshots, he started to bring coffee and after two or three months of doing this, he started to get to know the young woman. He became a recognizable, friendly face.

Then one day she asked if he could play the saxophone because they might have an opportunity for him that afternoon. He lied, said yes, and then went out and used the last of his savings to buy a saxophone. Now, this isn't something I'd recommend you do, it's definitely a risk, but for him, it landed him his first role.

He had made his way into Hollywood and would become one of the band members in the film *Ray,* which would later go on to win an Academy Award. A good impression, a sense of passion, a pinch of persistence, and the willingness to be ready to jump on board and say yes when the opportunity arises are the ingredients you need to combine with your knowledge and skills to get your shot in this industry.

But really, no matter what it is, the more you know and the more you can do, the more desirable you will become. Actors wind up becoming directors; musicians wind up becoming producers. Talent is always evolving as long as you're willing to learn. To me, the definition of a successful person is someone willing to learn as much as they can about the industry that they're working in.

This isn't exclusive to the entertainment industry, but you never know when things will be useful. That little bit of information about casting, writing, or even lighting might not be valuable today. But maybe two or three years from now, all of a sudden, someone asks the question, and you can reach in and pull out that little nugget of information.

For myself, my experiences running my own business in the hospitality industry and franchising in the entertainment industry have left me with a wealth of skills that are somewhat circumstantial. But they have helped me to build connections.

I've seen companies who haven't formatted their marketing correctly for mobile. They only have it formatted for wide screens, and I've reached out to them just to let them know. I don't expect anything from it, but I always like to think if the marketing for VIP Ignite was being cut off or contorted between devices, that someone would let me know. It's a way to share knowledge, and it's a way to start a dialogue.

If you have the skills, you'll always stand out, and when you stand out, you'll always be able to find a way in. But if you don't have the skills, you don't have to spend lots of money to get them. One of the actors we work with had a role on *Days of Our Lives*. It was one of his first roles and for the audition; they were looking for someone who could juggle and shuffle poker chips.

At the time, he didn't have a clue how to do it, but he bought himself a set and went to YouTube and learned a few tips and tricks from videos so that he could bring something else to the audition. He wasn't great, but he could do it. And when he went to the audition, he was the only one who could. It got him the role, just because he could embody the character that little bit more than everyone else around him. There is value in what you can teach yourself because you really don't know when the UNvaluable becomes INvaluable.

TRANSFORMING WHAT YOU HAVE

The first thing we do is look at how you are already presenting yourself. Email is a good place to start, and it's something that people are becoming more and more conscious of these days. Having a divide between personal and professional, making sure that before you even have the chance to make the first impression in person, the first impression in the online space is just as good.

Make sure that you have a professional email, for example, rather than using a personal email for professional correspondence. No one is going to know who BootyLicious74@hotmail.com is from a first glance and even though it's something that you'd likely use as a kid, it's not the impression you want to give as an adult.

In a similar sense, you want to make sure you're keeping your face on social media while being conscious about what you're posting, being in the public eye. What are the first things people see when they look to follow you on the likes of Instagram or TikTok? Are you posting randomly or is there a purpose to what you're posting? You want to make sure that, while your social media can be personal, you don't want it to be detrimental should you enter the public eye. As an example, you shouldn't be making posts about skipping work or calling in sick after a late night. You want to show you have a good work ethic if you decide you want to post about work.

Your social media is a great way for people to get an insight into your personality and what kind of things you get up to. It's an amazing tool to tell a narrative, so what we try to do, once we see what's already there, is to magnify the more intriguing parts of the narrative. A lot of the time, people don't know how interesting they are. They struggle to tell me ten interesting things about themselves, usually after the second or third thing on their list.

An example that comes to mind is when I was speaking to one of our first models. When I asked her to tell me something interesting about herself, she said there wasn't anything. So, I took it from another perspective and asked what she did for a living. She talked about working in the Navy as a combat fighter pilot. With all this experience at sea and in the air, I was just dumbfounded. How could she not think that this was interesting?

Most people do not see their day-to-day as interesting. What one person finds interesting may be normal for someone else. For this model, being a combat fighter pilot wasn't new or exciting. It was just what she did to earn money. Though for me, hearing her story was fascinating.

I can see the *amazing* in people's daily lives just because I'm not familiar with them. Baristas at Starbucks, for example, can handle customers in high-pressure situations. They've got to be fast-acting and on point, focusing on their skills to get every order right. These are things you can twist and talk about in interviews to make yourself interesting.

EXPANDING YOUR RESUME WITH VIP IGNITE

You can never know everything in the entertainment industry. Whether you're an actor, model, musician or even working behind the scenes, there is always something else you can learn. What can be difficult, however, is finding the opportunities that will give you those new skill sets.

That is part of the purpose of VIP Ignite. We connect you with people who can give you these skill sets, people who can take you to the next level and help you become successful in your career. Our speakers share their experiences with you, which gives you access to the tips and tricks that they learned on the way to becoming successful in the industry, no matter what industry that might be. We also host events where you get more than a lecture from a speaker on a stage. You get hands-on experience with what our speakers share by putting it into practice. That experience becomes something you can then add to your resume.

We put together an event in Atlanta for stage combat training and it was amazing. We hired the head of stunts for *Fear the Walking Dead,* which was absolutely incredible. He has about thirty years of experience in the business, has traveled the world, worked on some of the biggest movies, and has dedicated his career to safety on set. Our talent was able to attend the event and learn how to use prop weapons on a set with one of the legends in the business.

At the time we were planning this event, there was that tragedy on the movie set with Alec Baldwin. It left people asking the question, how could something like that happen when you have so many people on set who are trained, and yet a mistake still took place? So, we decided that even though we would still do a scene with the prop weapons, we would add an extra day to also show our talent what it was like to handle real weaponry. I wanted the talent to understand what a real weapon felt like, so there would be less of a chance that they would make those mistakes. We brought them to a live shooting range and brought in a professional instructor who taught them to handle the weapons safely.

It was an incredible weekend where, not only did they get to have stunt and combat training, but by the end of the weekend, they also understood that being able to handle even a prop is their responsibility. They learned to never put a prop weapon into someone else's hands without knowing it was safe. They also learned that if they were handed a weapon, they would personally know how to make sure that it was safe—even if someone else had already told them that it was safe.

That weekend, we did a scene where we coordinated an entire stunt routine that was like a drug cartel–SWAT team standoff. Half the group was playing the cartel henchmen, with one of them in the role of the head of the family. The other half was playing the SWAT team that had come to raid the Kingpin's lair.

There was a lot of fighting going on, where the talent was working with prop guns and weapons. They had to learn how to fall and die correctly, how to take a hit and make it look real. There were all these little nuances that you wouldn't even think about, like how to throw a punch and roll with the punches while making everything look real on camera. It's something that I think everyone feels like they'd be able to do, but it's not that simple. There's a technique behind it, a skill set that you have to learn.

We organize so many amazing weekends for our talent, but I think that event was one of our best. It was so incredible because it was important. We were able to send those ripples of knowledge out, while giving people an opportunity they likely never would have been able to have. Now our talent knows they can handle weapons safely, they have connections that can make an impact, and they have something that will really stand out on their resume when they walk into a room.

INTERVIEWS FROM THE INDUSTRY, PART FIVE

Robert Galinsky
Head of Robert Galinsky Coaching, TED and TEDX Talk Speaker

At a recent VIP Ignite event, we did an incredible exercise with an amazing teacher and artist, Laurie Carlos, that was all centered around "chemistry." We worked on developing chemistry. We focused on getting the clients and students to understand what chemistry is, so that when they're on set or trying to get on set, they would have a better sense of how to relax and be themselves, and how to elicit that in other people too. When you can do that, then you can let that chemistry develop into whatever the next great thing is. You make real connections that can help you on and off set.

We don't give lectures. It's an exercise workshop where you get hands-on experience, going through the motions as if you were already there on a set trying to do these things. I think for this event we had around 30 clients: they got some instructions and went on a very short walk-about, then they came together, got some more instructions, and set to work. By the end, they took everything they had observed in that initial walk-about, and worked together, building their chemistry. They turned it into a short live performance of award-winning quality.

But what's the kind of chemistry we're talking about?

Well, it's the kind where you open up and click with other people. It's the kind of connection that you have with people that you're familiar with, as well as the connection you make with strangers you've never met before. It's about knowing how to make those interactions as comfortable as possible so that you can work on whatever the task at hand is.

Charles Bodner
BRS/Gage Talent Agent

I'm an agent and if I'm at the theater, or I'm at a party or something, sometimes people start talking to me about their career. I'm very polite about it. I'll talk about it for a little bit, but if it goes on and on and on, then I'll just say, here's my card, send me your info. Send me a picture and resume with a short, nice cover letter about what you've done or the roles that you booked, and maybe that you know someone who's my client or someone that's a casting director. That's important, too.

Your cover letter should be concise and not three pages long. It should say what you've just done if you're doing something now, and what you're looking for as an actor. I don't need to hear that you're great or did the Wizard of Oz. Tell me what you're doing now, that you're the lead in a play, or working on this production in a local theater, anything. But it's got to be worth it.

You've got to network, but there is a time and a place, so remember that. But I also say you've got to be ambitious. If you don't say something, you'll miss out. You got to take advantage of a situation.

If you're going to invite an agent to see your work, it's got to be something professional and something that you're proud of, to make us interested. If it's not, we're not going to sit through it. Then we're going to get angry—that's our Friday night too. If you invite us to things that are not very well-produced, and we get down there, we're sitting on folded chairs in a closet and it's 900 degrees in there, it's like, "NO!"

If you're not working on something you're proud of, wait till the next one. Wait until you get something else. I'd much rather you wait to get something else, than have me come down and see you in something bad because there goes my opinion of you. It's done.

That's also why I say to an actor when they audition: if you're not prepared, don't go. Especially don't go if it's your first time with a casting office because that's the way they're going to remember you. They're going to say you're terrible. If, God forbid, something happened and you couldn't prepare the material or something, just say to them, "Listen, can we reschedule?" And if not, then you should wait for the next one. Another opportunity will always arise if you're proactive and persistent.

Pat Addiss

Our Fairy Godmother, Jiminy Cricket, and Mary Poppins all in one, Broadway Producer and Broadway Expert

This business is very, very tough, and very competitive, and unless you are driven and it's your passion, you will never make it to the top. It is filled with stories about how people made it and it sounds very, very easy, but it isn't easy at all. You've got to be in top form today. It used to be years ago, a singer who danced knew it all, or a dancer who sang knew it all. Now I need more. You have to sing. You have to dance. You have to act. It really is that competitive.

I had an intern once who was very, very gifted. She would get up at four in the morning, to put her name on the list for an audition that she may or may not get to do. She was driven and she was going to make it. She would try out for everything she could. She did stuff as a child, and she is a dancer, singer, and actress. She became an assistant choreographer. She put her foot in every door she could and got to know everyone she could. That's the other half of the battle.

I'm all about networking. You must network today. It is so important to meet and keep in touch with people. I don't always get to work with new talent because I'm not a casting director or an agent. I have had the chance to meet some new talent once in a while when I've done readings that I cast myself or help cast with somebody, but most of the time I will work with somebody that I know.

This might seem unfair to people starting in the industry. I say to you, "Get to know people," but then I say, "I only work with people I know." So how are you ever going to get to know me, for example, if I've never worked with you and won't work with you unless I've worked with you before? How do you get in the door? How do you make people notice you? It is tough. It really is, but that's true of any business or career.

You have to do readings and do everything that you can to possibly get into them. You have to check out all the different things online that tell you where auditions are. Audition, audition, audition, and take lessons. The old joke about how do you get to Carnegie Hall? Practice, practice, practice. You have to be skilled in your craft. You can't just go in there and not be prepared. If you're auditioning for something, do as much preparation as possible. If there's a video, watch the video. Learn the part that you're auditioning for. Be as prepared as you possibly can be.

I did a little bit of the casting when I was on *The Fantasticks*. I remember we were always looking for young, new talent for that and I was appalled by how girls came in to try out for Louisa in *The Fantasticks*, who is a very old-fashioned, lovely '90s girl. Girls would come into an audition in these little, skinny, strapless dresses and they'd spend half the time pulling the top up and the bottom down. That was inappropriate. So, always think about what you wear to an audition, and think about the part you want to play.

Do as much preparation as possible. Don't think you can just "wing it" because you can't anymore. There are too many other better prepared people out there. Too much of the competition is extremely well-prepared. If you don't get something but you've done an outstanding audition, the people in the room will remember you for something else. I recommend people all the time. I love to connect with people and I'm always getting people jobs or interviews and things because that's personally what I love to do.

Patrick Quagliano

Head of Stella Adler, Acting Coach of the Stars

It doesn't take a license to be an acting teacher. You don't have to pass a test. Anyone can just put a shingle out and say, "I am a teacher," but not everyone is qualified to be one. I certainly don't like to be critical of peers, but some of these people who represent themselves as teachers have no experience, so you have to be very careful.

First, reach out to a reliable studio. A reliable studio will not hire unqualified teachers. After you've been to a studio, identify the teachers you have chemistry with and work with them.

I'll tell you one way I wouldn't go about it, which may surprise you. I think the fact that people say they work with famous actors, in my view, means nothing because I have seen such a misrepresentation of that. I know teachers who name-drop all kinds of names, but you have no idea whether it is true or not because that is just what they are all about: meeting people and dropping their names. All those teachers talk about is themselves and the people they've taught and the people they've worked with. The teaching you end up getting from them is lousy.

I know one particular very famous teacher who will be unnamed, but when I was a young actor, he had the most fascinating stories about everybody. I assumed they were true, but I learned nothing but the stories about everybody he knew. On my website, you won't find the names of any actors I have taught. I hope my website speaks for itself and that my classes and what I do in my classes also speak for themselves. I don't think name-dropping is the way to go about it.

Another way to find a teacher is through word of mouth. Go to an actor you know you like. Go to someone whose work you like and admire or they're a friend of yours and ask them who they studied with. That is actually how I get most private coaching: the students I have taught before telling others to study with me.

You should expect a teacher to teach you the craft and to appreciate the fact that growth as an actor and growth as a human being are synonymous. I put a lot of responsibility on teachers and the things they are teaching. I think that you should look for a teacher that can not only contribute to and awaken you to the craft of acting but can awaken you to a new way of looking at yourself and the world.

The Stella Adler technique, which I teach, has three parts to it. It begins with Foundation, which has all the tools that ground you with those ingredients that you need to be able to work as an actor: working with the imagination, understanding the value of circumstances, how to play actions, and the importance of justification in the process. Those are all the tools that ground you in the technique.

The second part is Character: the development of the actor as a character. Since you are dealing with characters that act and react in the present, you have to have the ability to create a past that justifies emotionally why the character does what they are doing in the present. You need to be able to detach yourself and call upon the thoughts, feelings, and actions of the character, not yourself. You are the instrument you need to perform your craft, so when you play a character, you must develop the resources to hone your instrument to truly embody and portray the character.

And the third part of it is Script Interpretation: when you have your foundation, once you have all your tools, and you can play characters, then you have to put yourself in the dramatic or comedic framework of a script or screenplay. It is knowing how to break down scripts, how to take words on a page and translate them into human experience, and into playing a character who is a version of that experience. It is amazing, and it all comes from an actor reading words on a page written by the playwright.

My goal is to be a teacher comfortable with all three portions of the technique: Foundation, Character, and Script Interpretation. I will tell you that I feel I am almost there.

Many others feel that I am already there. But I think that there is more development ahead; we are always developing.

Thomas G. Waites
Director, Producer, Writer

A lot of people make the mistake of putting the cart before the horse. They're all into networking, but really what's the point of networking if someone says, "Well, okay, go ahead, show us what you've got. Do a monologue. Do a scene," and your only response is to admit you don't know how to do any of these.

Well then, you obviously haven't read enough, have you?

You need to be reading a new play every week if you want to be an actor. That's what I did, and I found parts that were dead on right for me. I used those parts to get into the Actors Studio again, where I made invaluable connections and relationships. Yeah, you can't get into the Actors Studio the first time out. I did, but only because I had the craft and a lot of experience. By twenty-nine, I'd already been on Broadway several times, and I'd done several motion pictures, so I had a lot of skill and determination, and people could see that when I walked into a room.

But if you can't get in as an actor right away, you do it the Michael Imperioli way— you work as an intern. Michael's a very lovely man, by the way. He was an intern when I was at the Actors Studio. He was mopping the floors but was watching and studying everything around him, and then he became a big star on *The Sopranos*. He put the work in and got the result. It works through work because work gets work.

I had this affliction, and I think many of us have something similar. It's that thing that just gets in our way. For some people it's alcohol, but for others, for example, it's weight, or it's food. They have food issues, and it gets out of control, then they wonder why they can't get hired as an actor.

Look in the mirror.

If you're 5'8" and nearly 200 pounds, then you're probably too heavy. You need to get conditioned, and you may not like hearing that, and maybe the world doesn't like hearing that. I'm not trying to shame anyone. I'm just telling you how it is. You don't have to be ripped, but you have to be healthy. It's business. It's dependent upon the way you look. You're asking people to stop what they're doing, to look at you and give you their attention, but if you don't take care of yourself, why should they look at you?

I have to train every day. I wake up at 5:00 every morning and I do Wim Hof breathing. I put my feet in ice for fifteen minutes. I run four miles. I do 200 push-ups and 200 sit-ups and I'm sixty f-ing seven years old. And I tell you what, I hate every second of it, but I do it because I want to be the greatest. I want to be the greatest writer and director in the world. That's my drive, that's my ambition. I'm not there yet, but I will get there.

Haviland Stillwell

Multi Hyphenate Actress, Singer, Producer, Director, Writer

Working with VIP Ignite is like a component of producing for me.

Producing, for me, is very much about bringing forth and helping to guide a project from start to finish. A lot of times it's a project that I'm also involved in as an actor or singer, or something else. I enjoy that because I like being involved with so many facets of a project. I find coaching to be very similar.

When you're coaching, you're giving people hope; you're helping them to realize their dreams. When they're stuck, you're offering them support and encouragement to help them push through and keep going. You're helping them get over whatever they're having trouble with and unlock a new skill or new potential that they maybe didn't think they had or could do. I find that I really love coaching. It's being able to give something back, but it is also a two-way street.

It's inspiring for me to work with people at all levels. I learn so much from extremely famous and successful actors; it is so exciting just to be in their presence. But in the same way, someone who is starting completely from scratch and is just getting into the industry has that drive and fire in them. They're so enthusiastic about everything. They're not sure what to do next, so they're just looking for support and some guidance to navigate the path they're on.

Honestly, I think that the world could use a lot more of that enthusiasm. There's so much negativity in the world that it's nice to see when people are earnestly and enthusiastically supportive of each other. As an actor, I crave that support, but it's not always easy to get.

When you're a teenager or a young adult, everybody expects that you don't know anything. You're so new to it that there aren't as many expectations put on you. By the time I was a young adult and I'd been working in the industry for over a decade, I was still considered to be new. I was working on Broadway in these very high stake, commercial platforms. I was on top of my job, but I still felt like it was okay if I asked for advice from people. I felt like I could ask for help and get support because nobody thought of me as an "expert."

I think that the older you get in this industry, the harder it becomes to not only get support but also to ask for it. When you get older, people expect you to be an expert. It's almost as if you're supposed to know everything the moment you turn thirty, but we all know that's just not true. People just assume that you know more—or that you know what you're doing in the first place—and it becomes harder to reach out and say that you need help.

It doesn't matter how old we are. In this industry, we're always learning.

People who don't work in this industry might have a new job every five years or so. But for us, we have a new job every other week. We are constantly in a new work environment surrounded by new bosses, new co-workers, and new collaborators. So, when you start a new job, you need to learn so many new things, and as an artist, you have to constantly learn these things over and over again each time you're on a new set working in a new genre with a new company.

It takes a lot of bravery and courage to ask for help and support when you're older. I think the expectation in this industry that you should know what you're doing at a certain age makes no sense. You're expected to learn new things all the time. If you're not asking questions, then you're wasting time. Every question you ask is an opportunity to go deeper, to connect with more people, to learn more, and to learn how to do better work.

Ryan Colby
Head of Ryan Colby Management

No matter what field of the industry they're in, everyone understands that when you're on a set, there are time constraints. You can't just sit there all day. It's more important than talent.

Staying on schedule is something that I try to do, and I think I do it well. If I say we're going to be done by six o'clock, then come 6:01 everything will have been concluded, packed up, and we'll be done for the day. When you're on the clock, you need to make sure that you're making every second count because that ensures that everything keeps moving for everyone on set.

I was a model for fifteen years. I've been on hundreds and thousands of sets, and I've never been on a working set where this was not pushed. Your hair, your makeup, and your wardrobe all have to be done for each shoot, and it has to be done on time because we need to finish on time, right? If you're shooting twenty, thirty, forty looks in a day, and they say it needs to be done by five o'clock, then it needs to be done by five o'clock. You might be able to finish early, but there is no chance that you can finish late.

It was something that I learned early on in my career. So now, as a manager and a coach, it's just something I inherently do. I keep time and I keep the train moving. And now it's kind of like blinking.

Robert Funaro

The Sopranos (2001-2006), Actor, TV Actor

When I was first acting on TV, I finally started to have fun when I let go of trying so hard to be good. The important thing is the work. Once you have learned your craft through the experience of working, and you keep on working, the important thing in the industry, I think, is to have humility. No matter where you're going, be gentle and kind, not arrogant.

Young actors on set are always going to see how hard things can get, but don't be discouraged. It isn't any different from any other job. It has the same things: people who are good at what they're good at and they do their job. Your job is to be prepared and to give it your best.

I said earlier that *The Sopranos* was my first real professional job. I didn't have an agent; the only thing I had was a high work ethic and some experience from doing a play called *A Streetcar Named Desire* with James Gandolfini. We were friends while we were in Scandinavia for three months. We came back; we parted ways, and we met maybe once after we came back from doing the tour of *Streetcar*.

We didn't really keep in touch. Jimmy went out to LA. He trained out there and became semi-successful, and, so of course, when he did *The Sopranos,* he was ready for it.

Years later, he found out from a friend of mine where I was working. There was a role that he thought I was right for, and he came to ask me if I was willing to audition. He also asked me if I had been acting and I lied. I said yes. Two weeks later I was on *The Sopranos*. It was my first professional gig, and it was quite nerve-wracking. It's not what people think. It is one thing to audition for the job and another when you're actually doing the job.

There's a process to acting—it's getting the work and then delivering. It's almost like being a racehorse. He gets entered into the race because he's good enough to race, then he has to race. Now, he might come in first and have a good race, he might come in third or fourth, or he might come in last. But he'll be entered again because he *got into* a good race.

I'm using that as an analogy to myself: I didn't come in first on the first season; it was very negligible. I mean, I had a wonderful time doing it, but it was very constricted because

I had not done it professionally before. So as far as my "apprenticeship", it was a great experience, and as I developed on the show, I was given more.

When I was starting out, I wish people had said to me, "There's a handful of great acting instructors in New York, and if you want to learn acting you should go to them," or get into a two-year program, or whatever, to learn acting. I wish I had read more about other actors and who they worked with, then sought those teachers.

I started in college and there's nothing wrong with going to college. You just do it. It was a great experience. Then, after college, you should look for someone, a mentor of some sort.

I wish I had been a little bit more knowledgeable or been around more people who knew what they were doing. If I was starting now, I would talk to people who were in the industry and read as much as I could. I would try to get into a program and take classes. You don't want to waste any time. It's a tough game, but you have a better chance if you bond yourself with people–trainers—who have a good success rate.

So how do you find trainers with a success rate?

I'm gonna make another horse racing analogy. You have to look at their "stable" of actors (their stable of horses). Have they had successful horses that have won the Kentucky Derby? Have they had any actors that have won Academy Awards? Even through word of mouth, what are people saying about them? Having that knowledge is important. If you look at the stable of actors they produce, then you'll see their worth. This is what actors who are starting out need to know.

Jesse Heiman

Actor, The World's Greatest Extra

It sounds silly, but I got into acting just by signing up for extra work in Berkley, California. If you want to be an actor, if you want to be an extra, you just sign up for extra work. You register for it and there's a process you go through. You have to fill out paperwork and submit photos and when you're right for a role, they'll call you for it. I just happened to work a lot. In my first year, I must have worked on hundreds of projects. I stuck to it. I just enjoyed doing it. I enjoyed everything: working on a different set or in different environments, working for different directors, working on films, working on commercials, working on TV shows, or just videos. I was doing anything and everything I could do. I really enjoyed just getting hands-on.

As I became more recognizable in the background, I started working more towards getting an agent and getting into SAG and getting more speaking parts rather than extra work. I recognize that there are a lot of people within the industry who frown on doing extra work as a way to become an actor. But I think it's a great tool for someone getting started, especially someone like me.

I didn't study any theater in college or participate in any plays in high school or anything like that. I originally came out to L.A. to be a writer and I'm still writing things, but I've never had anything made. I have a couple of scripts written that are done, but nothing's been green-lit or published yet. I'm still working on these things but acting has become my main focus. When I first started working as an extra, it was about just working for the money and making ends meet in L.A. I just took what I could take at the moment so I could pay rent.

As I became more in tune with meeting people throughout

the industry, they would call me back with multiple projects. That's kind of how the industry works. You end up working with the same people over and over, and if they like you and your personality, then they'll remember you. That's the reputation I got—that I was very happy-go-lucky, easy to work with, and very professional, so people wanted to work with me. I would actually go around to different sets as an extra and people would recognize me and want to work with me. That's amazing to me.

It's a small world, but it's not as small as you think. I mean, the majority of the SAG actors now have done some form of extra work at some point. It's a great way for everyone to get started. I don't know if there was one specific moment when I realized acting had become my career, but I think it was just when people kept using me. People kept using me and putting me right in the center of the shot and telling me that this was something I should be pursuing.

I took classes; I started looking for agents, and I started researching all I could about it. I became as informed about the industry as I could and really focused on becoming a better actor, not just an extra. Then, as I became a better actor, more opportunities came in and I felt more confident with my ability. I decided to pursue this, not just as a way to pay the bills, but as a career.

Santino Fontana

Tony-Award Winning Actor, Voice of Prince Hans (Frozen, 2013), V Actor, Broadway Actor

I think auditioning is like a necessary evil in a way that you just have to deal with. I think the quicker you can turn it into something fun, is the biggest trick. Figure out a way to flip it around in your head. I know that's hard to do because it's different for every audition. Some material you come across is easier to find a way to have fun with than others. There are some auditions you go to where you're miserable and you don't want to be doing it. Odds are, though, those are the ones you get because you're not trying to get them. I think it's kind of an exercise in randomness.

There are so many things that don't make sense about auditioning. It's not the most efficient way to find out if someone can act because it's nothing like any circumstance you're going to be in when you get the job. There's really nothing like it. There're no other actors. There's no rehearsal. There's no discussion about what you're trying to do. It's not really what it's going to be like. That said, if you can find a way to tap into something that's going to be fun for you, then that's the best way to look at it because it never stops.

I know really well-respected actors in their fifties who say it's a constant battle. An agent told me once that you have to think of it as their loss, that you don't need the job. It took me a while to get what she was saying. You want to be a working actor, but if you don't get something, that's kind of *their* loss. It's fine because, obviously, that wasn't where you were supposed to go. Remember: there's always going to be more auditions. Don't get caught up on that one opportunity that you missed.

I used to think that if I didn't get booked, then that was it. It was the end of the line, but that's not true. Opportunity is always knocking. You just have to keep listening for it. I don't think that the rejection ever stops either. Some people get to stop auditioning, but that's becoming less and less true over time, I think, for everybody.

A friend of mine who is a well-known actress told me she still auditions. I was shocked. There are actors and actresses who have been nominated for Emmys, for big awards, who still audition. I remember I attended an audition once and one of them walked into the room right before me!

Auditioning is a necessary evil and one that never really goes away, so we might as well make the most of it!

CHAPTER 7

DOWN TO THE BUSINESS OF THE BUSINESS

If you can learn to add value to other people's lives first and expect nothing in return, it's amazing how many doors will open for you.

— *Bill Walsh*

What if your dreams suddenly came true? how would you deal with the ups and downs of a capricious industry? How would you be realistic but remain positive? It's certainly not easy. You have to make sure you are making good financial decisions, along with planning for a career that will have longevity while maintaining the drive and passion that got you into the business in the first place. Once you have some understanding of the business side of the business, it becomes a lot easier to keep your momentum.

When most people start this journey, they don't have access to the information, or the connections, they need. But it's when you have those resources at your disposal that suddenly everything becomes so much easier. For example, it's like going to a Tony Robbins event. You listen to what he has to say, think about the things he's talking about. Soon you start to think about those things too—factoring in his explanations and reasoning until the road clears and a new path opens.

There are a lot of people who feel like they've made up their minds about how this industry works. They think that because they know a lot about their part of the industry; they have an understanding of it all. I've had a few instances where my colleagues and I have had young women on the other end of the phone call who can recite, to the number and letter, their physical attributes, from their height to their hair color, as well as their dreams of becoming the world's next supermodel. However, the problems always came when we started to ask more questions. They would repeat the same things over and over again. These women knew they wanted to be in the industry, but they didn't know how to express it other than by using the words and phrases they thought we wanted to hear.

If you're not familiar with the industry or are among the aspiring talent looking to get your foot through the door, you're likely not going to understand a lot of the jargon that gets thrown around. Think about it this way: if you were a specialized attorney, you would understand all the different types of law, but the people around you likely have a fixed mindset about you and what you do. Depending on their economic level in life, they might even look at you as being one of the most helpful people in the world or one of the worst.

How do you become a specialist? Lawyers and attorneys study for years to know all they know, but there isn't really anything like that for the entertainment industry. There are courses you could take and lectures you could attend to become more knowledgeable and skilled in such things, but in the end, does that make you a specialist?

It might, but you'll likely only know about the one area in which you've been trained. You won't know about all the other different areas of the entertainment industry. That's where VIP Ignite comes in. What we do is help aspiring talent, who not only want to be discovered but who also want to become specialists, to grow their careers.

Now, I've already discussed the dark side of the online world of the entertainment industry, and you've probably seen the adverts looking for people to star in indie films or participate in freelance photo shoots on the likes of Instagram and Facebook.

More often than not, these are the kind of adverts that only appear because the algorithms have noticed that you search for terms like modeling, creative, writing, film, acting, and singing. They grab your interest and attention, but when you dive further, you have to register for a hidden service and pay a hidden fee before you'll even be considered for the position. It's likely you'll never hear from them again, or if you do, it'll be an empty apology as you're told the fees are non-refundable. You can find the same thing in abundance on Craigslist.

You can take a chance with adverts you find online. I mean, in the beginning, that's where I started looking for people to attend the event which first launched VIP Ignite, but at the end of the day, it's still a chance, a risk. A hundred doors might get slammed in your face before a single one opens, and you might face hundreds of roadblocks before you discover a single open road, and for some, that is enough to turn them away from the industry entirely.

You're only going to build real relationships and credible

connections by going out to the places and spaces where these people actually are. You need to have the drive to put yourself out there and be willing to make those connections on your own merit. That comes back to the passion you have for being a part of this industry. Now, that doesn't mean flying out to Hollywood and trying to mingle with producers and directors in the hopes of getting your big break because there is a good chance you won't even know who those people are.

What I mean is to use the avenues available to you right now. Go online to follow them on social media, comment on their posts, share their work and ideas, and when you see they're going to be speaking somewhere or attending an event as a famous face, go there to see them and maybe even meet them.

There's a reason I dubbed VIP Ignite the "second secret" to your success in the entertainment industry. Once you have found your footing, having that persistence necessary for surviving and the passion for thriving, we'll work to help you build more relationships and give you more credible connections. You've started to plan your journey, plot those points on your map, and with VIP Ignite you'll have the kick-start you need to make the legwork so much easier.

HAVING A HELPING HAND

After hosting hundreds of events, I started noticing something and saw an opportunity to not only expand VIP Ignite but also expand the help that we could offer to our talent and clients. What I noticed was that there were so many people in the United States just looking to find their footing in this industry. People who were being expected to make the transition into the larger market without having the experience or confidence to do so.

I noticed that the way the smaller boutique agencies generated income wasn't through placing their talent in jobs. They were instead selling the chance for professional photo shoots or offering classes. Even though there is nothing wrong with this mode of business and it's a necessary part of the industry, it doesn't really give you the best insight into how the business works.

These agencies operate in a smaller market and therefore don't have access to higher-level photographers, for example. The experience they offer is valuable but it's a micro-version of the industry, an almost watered-down version of how it really works. They're not always at the forefront, so they don't always have the best access to news and information regarding the industry.

That's what got me thinking. We were inviting talent to these events where people at the forefront of their careers came to speak and share information and knowledge. So why couldn't we represent the talent as well?

We decided to act as a "mother agency" for a lot of the talent who came to our events. That way, we would take responsibility for them and set them on the right path. A "mother agency" is kind of like your mom: they are the ones who are going to put the most time, energy, and effort into seeing your career thrive.

As a mother agency, we get involved and make sure you keep having new destinations on your journey to success because, for a lot of the actors, models, and musicians signed with big agencies, there is very little guidance and interaction. With big agencies, you can quickly become another name on their roster. Essentially, unless a client is looking for someone who fits your exact qualifications or description, you'll likely never get a call. What we wanted to do was create an up-to-date and interactive database for clients to find talent quickly and easily that didn't pigeonhole or marginalize those we represented.

Truth Management was launched during the COVID-19 pandemic, and since its launch, it has had explosive growth. The film industry has undergone huge changes as a result of the pandemic, but that has only benefited Truth Management and the talent we represent.

Hollywood is no longer the epicenter of the film industry. Studios are moving closer to home and organizations are shifting locations across the United States. Films are being shot in Louisiana and Detroit instead of in a Hollywood warehouse, and so many films are being worked on with smaller and smaller budgets. So now, who do people call when it comes to casting extras?

If you're no longer in that epicenter, then it's suddenly going to cost more to bring extras from Hollywood to shoot in Detroit, for example. There's nobody representing people by the thousands. The agencies that do exist might only represent a few hundred people. There are few options available for fast and easy hires and that's why, all of a sudden, Truth Management has become so popular. It is an international database that people can call upon to find available talent almost instantly.

Before Uber, you had to stand on the street corner trying to hail a cab, right? Now, with Uber, everything has suddenly been put in your hands and your control. Gone are the days of waiting on a street corner and hoping a free cab drives by. You can now call up Uber and dictate the time and place for a driver to pick you up. I wanted Truth Management to become the Uber for talent.

I wanted to bring the company to a level of automation and security for our talent that not only gave them control over their careers but also increased its value to larger production companies. That way we could negotiate better rates with smaller production companies as well as work with bigger companies like Paramount and HBO.

As the company keeps growing, I want us to become the dominant force and maintain the momentum we have had over the pandemic. We've been working personally with some of the biggest agents and casting directors in the world. They are the ones who dictated what they wanted to see from talent in the database: from showing up on time to knowing availability beforehand, seeing a portfolio to seeing a film reel or listening to a demo. Just like our talent, they wanted full transparency with what was going on, so creating a system that did this ensured that both parties would always benefit from being a part of it. So, in addition to working with the people, we have also been fine-tuning our software to make it all happen smoothly.

INTERVIEWS FROM THE INDUSTRY, PART SIX

Charles Bodner
BRS/Gage Talent Agent

One of the challenges when you're "wanted" is that everybody's going to want you to do their project. You have to learn to be a little bit more selective when picking and choosing your projects. You need to know whether you want to slow-roll a film or whether you want to do a series.

Nowadays, a lot of actors that are on the rise don't want to sign for seven years for one series because it's a good portion of their life. They don't want to do the same thing for seven years. That means you have to be really picky about which series you're looking at and think about where you want to spend your next seven years.

When you're on the rise, there are certain things you can't do anymore. You can't do the smaller roles and you can't do something that's going to take you out of town for ten weeks. You've got to be a little more selective. It can be challenging to find great material because sometimes you get things thrown at you that are just not that great.

On the other hand, if you're on the rise and doing big movies with the likes of Spielberg, and your friend rakes in this gem of a play that's showing downtown in an independent theater, sure why not? It's six weeks, it ends in the summer, and nothing's going on, so you do it. It's a chance to strengthen those acting muscles, gain some more experience, and do something fun.

If you're doing big movies and all of a sudden someone calls and the casting director says they want this actress or actor to do a one-scene role in the next film, if it's for the likes of Martin Scorsese, then really, why not? If it's a small budget or a poor script, then maybe say no. It's not going to hurt your career. If anything, it's going to help it.

Once someone is on the rise, we're very selective, and it's not necessarily about the size of the role, it's about the quality of the role. Two lines in the background of a TV series, if you're a new actor, yeah, why not? Go for it. If you're at the stage where you're someone who's on the rise, who has done guest bookings, and a few of those central roles, you don't want to take that step backward. It might be a thousand dollars for the day, twelve hundred or fifteen hundred a day, and that's great, but you're not going to want the business to look at this series and see you and question why you did that. You really get nothing out of it besides the money.

If you need the money, if you need that injection, then we may not think you should go for it, but we're not going to stand in your way. There have been so many good and great actors who have taken bad roles because work is work, and money is money. But listen, everything you do is experience. For someone who is just out of school, three lines on a show is great. They're going to learn about the craft of TV, production, directing, and acting for television. That's like getting a paid learning experience!

Haviland Stillwell

Multi Hyphenate Actress, Singer, Producer, Director, Writer

I think the pandemic threw everybody for such a loop and, because of it, there have been so many changes, a lot of which are positive. There are so many things that have exploded over the past three years, like people's awareness of others, equal rights issues, racial issues, sexual orientation issues, and gender issues. All the rules have changed. Everyone is having to navigate the 'new now.' I think it's why we're all in need of a little support, no matter what path we're on.

A lot of times, the people who have inspired me have nothing to do with the industry I'm in. Somebody will say something that connects with me and that I can apply in my life and my job. Everything is a cycle. Being open to knowledge, and to giving and receiving from everyone, has been extremely valuable to me. It's been important not just for becoming successful in the entertainment industry but also just in enriching my life.

That's also what art is. It's about connecting and inspiring people even though they might have no actual connection to you. You can watch a film and have zero connection to the circumstances of the character, but on an emotional level, you can still relate to them, connect with them, and be inspired by them.

The tricky part of being a working artist is that sometimes you do things purely for income. That doesn't mean that you're not receiving really valuable information and inspiration that can help you move forward in your career. The whole job is about doing what you have to do and self-directing as much as possible. Then, when you're in your art environment, whether it be a stage, recording booth, film set, or whatever, you can be completely amenable and pliable to what the director is asking.

There are so many unknowns that you have to be able to manage, so the more skills you have, the more you know, and the better you'll be. That's how I coach. Learn your lines and learn the script. At the same time, learn everything you possibly can because you don't know who you're going to be working with. You don't know what they'll bring to the table, and you also don't always know what you're going to be doing.

You don't know if it's going to be 100 degrees and you might have to wear ten layers of clothes and a wool coat because you're supposed to be filming a winter scene. You don't know what's going to be going on around you, whether it's going to be loud or frantic or whether there will be other people in the background distracting you. There are so many things that you have to be really focused on and just be willing to roll with things, be creative, and keep things going.

I feel like part of acting school or modeling training should be a scene or shoot with the AC cranked to 60 degrees and you have to do a lingerie shoot, or a bikini shoot on the beach. You've got to pretend to be in love and that it's the best thing ever while you're absolutely freezing. You should also have to do scenes or shoots where the opposite happens. It's part of your job to be able to make these things look truthful. You have to make it work and at times, this is really what it's like.

Bill Walsh

CEO of PowerTeam International, America's Small Business Expert, Top Success Coach, Top Business Coach, Author

I think that before you do business with someone, you've got to like the person. That's the mistake people make as they try to lead with their business and think it's all business.

The thing is, most people think that when they come into a conversation in business, as an entrepreneur or even for those working in the entertainment industry, you have to negotiate. It has to be "Here's what I have and here's what I want," and you keep going until you find someone who can give you that. But if you do that, then you're going to need to be prepared to leave a lot of money on the table.

There are many people who don't realize that relationships are built one-to-one. Business is often done one-to-many, but if you don't invest in the relationships, then you're gonna miss the bigger picture of being able to build something so much greater together.

When you learn to add value to other people's lives first and expect nothing in return, it's amazing how many doors will open for you. Until you understand that concept, you'll always be tuned into a station called WIIFM—*What's In It For Me*. But if you tune into a different station, *What's In It For Them*, think about how you can serve the other person first, you can let the universe give its yield because it will yield the greatest dividends ever.

Everything is about frequency when you tap into those at a much higher level. And when you change the station you're tuned into, all of a sudden you're playing chess while everyone else is playing checkers. You're in a Formula One sports car when they're in a Yugo. They can't even see you go by, because you're so much more in tune with the people around you.

Go to Facebook and see how many "friends" you have on your friend list. Most of them are not your friends, or at least I wouldn't call them friends. They're acquaintances; they're social connections. I think in life you only have a few real friends.

How many friends do you have that you could text and say, "I need $5,000 by five o'clock today because I'm stuck with a medical emergency," who would actually try to step up and help you? Or how about sending a text saying, "Hey, I can't give you anything, but I really need a hand. Could you come give me a hand with work this week?" How many of your Facebook friends would give you their time for nothing just because you needed them?

It's always during the toughest times when you can find your real friends. And, in reality, you probably don't have a lot of friends like that. I think you can have social connections, you can have friends, but then you have your real friends. It's what I would call your inner circle. Those are the people that, if you were going through the toughest times, would be there for you in the blink of an eye, no matter the distance, to make sure you were okay.

Business can be a transaction, and that's okay. There needs to be some balance between your business relationships and your personal relationships. When you can work with people, make money, build a legacy together, and still become great friends, then that connection is priceless. You don't want to cross over by giving them advice that's not in your wheelhouse just because you see them as more of a friend than a partner. That's not going to help them.

I have business partners and friends who have become close personal friends, but I still don't try to give them relationship advice because that's just not in my wheelhouse. Stay in your lane, whether it's personal or business. If someone comes to me and asks about fitness, I'm not going to try to give them advice because I'm not a fitness coach, but that doesn't mean I won't help. I can connect them with someone who knows that space and can really help them because I have so many people in my good old-fashioned Rolodex that are great at what they do.

So don't start giving out advice on stuff you don't know about. If you care about people, you'll make those connections, those real connections, right away. The power of connections is in the one-to-one relationships, but then it hinges on the follow-up and the follow-through. Those connections might not always be able to help you, but by making the connection, you can at least open a door that otherwise would have never opened.

Santino Fontana

Tony-Award Winning Actor, Voice of Prince Hans (Frozen, 2013), TV Actor, Broadway Actor

A role has to excite me in some way. There has to be something that stands out to make me really want to go to bat for a character. That's usually what it comes down to. I have to want to tell someone's story, to do something that will be fun throughout, or that I want to work with people in the cast and crew. I'm always thinking about the last thing I did, and I don't want to feel like I'm getting into a rut or repeating myself. Variety is the spice of life, the fun part, and it keeps me stretching. It keeps me working and it also fuels me.

I remember when I had an audition for the cop for the *Shades of Blue* show. Someone asked if the role was right for me and that just made me want to do it even more. A similar thing happened when I did a play Off-Broadway called *Sons of the Prophet*, written by Stephen Karam. I played a sensitive, young, gay man in a very, very isolated part of Pennsylvania who was afraid of death. After that show, if you had told anybody that I was going to be cast as Prince Charming in *Cinderella* on Broadway, they would have thought you were crazy.

When I was doing the first reading of *Cinderella*, a casting director called my agent and asked if I was available for an audition. When she said no, their first thought after hearing I was playing Prince Charming, was that I was playing the prince in a darker version of the story. They had associated me at that time with heavier, more dramatic material. I understand that and it's something that never stops. People are always trying to define you, so you have to just let that become background noise and keep moving past it.

It took me a long time to feel comfortable in front of a camera. I did a web series called *Submissions Only,* that Kate Wetherhead and Andrew Keenan-Bolger created. They are also both theater actors and they weren't feeling like they were getting the television and film opportunities that they wanted. They asked if I wanted to join and, of course, I said I'd love to. When you do something like that with friends, you start to understand the vocabulary that's required to tell a story through the camera.

You need the experience of doing it. It couldn't be more different from on stage, where you have to use your whole body and your voice in a way that isn't natural. You have to understand your role from the beginning to the end.

In theater, you're the editor of your performance every night. Whereas, in camera stuff, your only job is to be truthful, honest, interesting, and spontaneous. That's your job, which is a completely different thing than crafting a performance from beginning to end.

You can do that in a film. You can't really do it on television unless you're a star or someone's going to help you do that because it takes time, and television works so much quicker than anything else. The turnaround is insane.

Learning to perform for a camera comes from just doing it so much that you can't do it anymore. Everything is different in front of a camera. It's really about that feedback of being able to see yourself and then learn from it. I made so many audition tapes to learn what is actually leading. I learned what is too much and what I can do less of by the sheer number of times doing it.

It's not easy to watch yourself. I mean, it's not hard for me now, but it wasn't easy at the beginning, and it's not for anybody. I have dear friends who are working actors who can't watch themselves, can't listen to themselves. They can't do it and they're doing fine.

I have always felt like it was something I had to do. I had to be able to see what I could do and what I couldn't. I feel that it's empowering to just jump in there and see it, so I can learn what I can and then move on. There's a lot of TV stuff I have done that I haven't ever watched. I don't typically watch things once I've shot them. It's not that I choose not to; I just don't go out of my way to watch it. I watch things more to get the job and feel comfortable with what I'm doing.

Sometimes it can be frustrating to watch the final product when you don't have any control over how it comes across to audiences. You shot it two months ago. You're not editing it, so you don't know which takes they're going to choose. You don't know what's important to the story. You don't have any control because they're trying to make it work best for the main character. You do know, typically, whether it's about you or not. If you're a guest star, you know it's not about you.

Years ago, I had an agent who represented me for voice-over work but never really sent me out for auditions. I had to bring it up with them before they started sending me out more. But then I talked to another friend of mine, who had done voice-over stuff in the past. She put me in contact with someone she knew who could *really* get me into the industry. They took me under their wing and taught me all they knew. It took me about three years doing about five to six auditions a week, without booking a single thing before I finally did it.

I gradually started doing some commercial voice-over stuff, but I was also in *Frozen* as one of the film's lead characters. It is two completely different styles of auditions, and it took a long time to develop the skills. It's the same thing as what I said about the camera stuff: you keep recording yourself, listening to it, learning how to make it better and what you need to do. You don't look back. You just keep going.

Nothing that we do is linear. Some people look at other people's careers and feel like because of their current success, their trajectory will just keep going up. But no matter who you are, or what you're doing, even if you're experiencing a high, your trajectory won't necessarily just keep going up. You know what I mean if you've experienced success; it really doesn't feel that way. It may look that way if you pick out certain moments, but it's not logical, and it's not linear. I think those are the two things that are the hardest to deal with.

Michael Stonewall Beaudry
Casting Director

People are unique and, depending on the person, you're going to have to approach each situation slightly differently. You have to remember that relationships are connections, and you have to start making connections to develop those relationships.

When I started, I was meeting and interacting with upcoming filmmakers and directors for music videos. I chased them because I had no one else to chase. I didn't concern myself with whether or not it would really turn into anything. I needed just one job. That was it.

When you get that one job, you have to nail it in the hopes they will hire you again or at least tell their friends about you. Then you keep hoping that, over the next year or two, you get a bunch of jobs from those beginning connections and relationships.

That's what happened to me.

I liked a couple of the guys I worked with. There was one woman I met who was really cool, and we became friends. That connection became a relationship, and eventually, when she was filming a music video, she asked me to cast it. I had zero doubt about my ability to do it. I was positive I could do it. And I was certain I could do it at least as well as anyone else doing it at the time.

It was a five, six-hour casting session. Half an hour into the casting, she was saying how great everything was going. After that, it all blew up in a great way. She recommended me to everyone, and I got more clients.

I worked really hard to be this fortunate. I worked as hard as humanly possible. The sacrifices I made were rough. I woke up at six am and came home at ten or eleven that night. I worked long days, one after the other, and did it for no money or sometimes even out of pocket for some jobs.

As a casting director, there's this transitional period where you go from running sessions and having a comfy little $1,000 to $1,300 per job to taking your own jobs. In the beginning, they will be for pennies, for literally zero, or even out of your own pocket. You also have to decide whether or not you want to take two or three steps back when you're broke.

A lot of my peers asked me how I did it and where I got my clients. Sometimes they would be up for jobs themselves, but they put in these outrageous bids, which I thought was weird because nobody knew who they were. They didn't have the credibility or the name yet. I didn't put in those kinds of bids because I figured if anybody was going to pay that kind of money, they would only pay that for an iconic casting director, right? They didn't want some new kid in their mid-to-late 20s, whether or not they're any good, shaping the look of their Fortune 500 company.

See, I would do a job in a studio as a session director for another casting director. Then at lunch, I would race to my car with my little mobile office and my mobile Wi-Fi, and I would start prepping my own jobs in secret for the next day. Then I would go back to finish the other job. When I finished that first job, I would rush to a restaurant, coffee shop, or even a bar at six, seven o'clock to finish my own work because it had to be done by eight. I still had a two-hour drive back home! I would do all these jobs in secret and then it all changed. Those jobs became more frequent and soon offered me more money, so it was all worth it.

In the beginning, I did a dozen jobs in a year. Then it was fifty or sixty jobs the next year. I started turning down all the session director jobs. I couldn't do it anymore because I was doing one hundred-thirty other jobs that year. And honestly, that was eight, nine years ago. It's been a blur since then. I've had just over eight-hundred jobs in the past four years, nearly two-hundred jobs a year. For some people that would be way too many, but for me, it has been incredible.

You have to be willing to put in that time, have that dedication, and sometimes it will be for nothing, because it's a little bit of a long game. But when you get it, it's awesome.

Tone Capone

A&R and Development, Vice President of Motown Records, Music Industry

There are a lot of opportunities out there. You've just got to know where to look and most new artists don't know where to look, so they try to figure it out as they go.

It's like anything else in life. You have to do your research.

You can't expect everything to come to you and for the label to find you on YouTube. There's more than a billion people on YouTube. It's not that they wouldn't appreciate your music; it's that your music is lost. You have to get it played somewhere where people are paying attention because when people are referencing you and people are highlighting who you are, that takes you to a different level.

You know what's funny to me? It's when artists press up t-shirts and give them out to generic people. It's just like, dude, you're throwing away money. That will do nothing for you. Be strategic. So, if you're going to spend money, instead of spending five hundred dollars on forty t-shirts, spend five hundred dollars and hire a publicist. Something like that.

Be smart. At the end of the day, what you have to understand as a new artist is that you have to invest in yourself. You're not going to get into the business for free. It's just not happening. You're going to have to spend money on studio time. You're going to have to invest in yourself, and that applies to anything. Many people just want to get t-shirts and this and that and all these little swag packets and school bags. If you're spending your money there, it's in the wrong place.

When you're a new business, you have to open a storefront; you have to invest in products; you have to invest in your security system; you have to invest in marketing and branding and this and that. Every business that operates today, that's open for business, is investing in itself to keep people coming and walking through the doors.

It's the same thing with an artist. If you want to keep building a fan base, you have to keep investing in yourself. Rihanna's album cost millions of dollars but she had to get the best producers. She had to get the best marketing people and the best radio people. She had to get the best of everything. That's why her album may cost five million dollars to make. The point is that five million is nothing if the album will generate ten million in revenue? You've got to look at it like that.

So, for a new artist who thinks, well, I don't want to pay for this and that, be realistic! At the end of the day, you're going to have to pay for something. You're going to have to pay for recording studio time. You're going to have to pay for a website. There are just certain things you're not going to get past. Get some great viral marketing or some search engine optimization for your site so that people notice you. Build your portfolio on platforms that get millions of views a day. Be in the right places, where the eyes are, and before you know it—well, you never know unless you try, right?

CHAPTER 8

LOOKING AT SUCCESS

I have worked with people from all walks of life, from C-Suite executives to young people in prison, and what I've found is that the principles are all the same.

It doesn't really matter what demographic we're working with, whether you're struggling in a jail cell or a boardroom: love is love, and creativity is creativity.

– Robert Galinsky

Everyone has a value. Everyone has an opportunity to be discovered. But everyone has to start some place, even if it's in the smallest of places.

I truly think success is one's ability to stay persistent, passionate, and persevere through the ups and downs. Take things slowly and be as informed and educated as you can be about what you want to do and what you want to achieve. The most successful people in the world are those who are constantly and eagerly learning from the people and the world around them.

When I meet somebody successful, I want to know what path they took to get there. I want to know their ups and downs, their trials and tribulations, and I want to celebrate with them when I finally understand how far they've come. Look at Pacino, for example. At the beginning of his career, he was sleeping on people's couches, moving from audition to job until finally, he figured it all out. Another example is Oprah. She started her career as a news reporter and now she owns her own network. They started small, with humble beginnings, and then they became great.

As much as their successes are something to marvel at, it's the ability to recognize the pattern of success that is one of the most beneficial things you can develop. What routes did they take to get to where they wanted to be? What did they have to do? What were their mistakes, the bumps in the road? What happened when they came to a roadblock and wanted to quit? What picked them back up? And most importantly, how did they learn all of this?

These are questions that VIP Ignite strives to answer. We want to be the fount of knowledge for our talent, bringing in those successful people to our events to pass on their secrets to success and relive their journeys for the benefit of the industry's up-and-coming. We want to be there when our talent starts their journey, stand with them at the start of the road and then cheer with them when they finally get to the end.

INTERVIEWS FROM THE INDUSTRY, PART SEVEN

Michael Stonewall Beaudry
Casting Director

I'm very, very proud of what I've done in my career.

CHAPTER 8 - LOOKING AT SUCCESS

I'm really proud of *This is America* for Childish Gambino, as an example.

Another thing I'm proud of doing was when I did "Immigrants (We Get the Job Done)" for the *Hamilton Mixtape*. That was awesome! It was for Lin Manuel Miranda, and it was one of those easy yes jobs. I made virtually nothing from it, but I would have paid out of pocket to do that one because it was Lin Manuel Miranda. How often does he decide to do something, and how often does that then trickle so far down that they ask *me* to be involved? So, we did this gigantic music video for it, and I cast it. It even won an MTV Music Video Award for Best Fight Against the System.

But in terms of a large number of jobs, I'm proud of the roles that I have been able to cast. I flipped a lot of the roles, from male to female, from white to black, and even booked transgender talent when they weren't looking specifically for a transgender actor. I worked with a bunch of Middle Eastern women in their early 20s to get their projects done. I'm proud of pushing to have a voiceover interface that has opened up voice acting to tens of thousands of new talent. And I'm proud of getting to add casting categories like non-binary and transgender, and even freckles and gapped teeth, because who would not want to include and represent these people and these things in people?

It's the right thing to do.

Alexandria De Rossi
The Firm LA Model & Talent Agent

I became an agent because it's what I aspired to be. I attempted it twice and failed. I let the industry as a whole intimidate me, but I'm here now, standing tall and I'm grateful. It was something that I was determined to do for myself and no one else but me. I knew I had the knowledge, skill, and business acumen to do this and be great.

Growing up, things were different. I was always told, "You're tall," "You're lanky," "You're not that attractive, no man's ever gonna want you," or "You've gotta try harder, do more to shine." But I never believed any of it. When people told me no, it just sparked something in me that meant I had to prove them wrong.

It's like a casting director once said to me, "Honey, you're not paying attention, it says no pitch calls. How many times are you gonna call?" And I just replied, "As many times as it takes until you take a closer look at my client."

No doesn't scare me, and that's the kind of person you have to be.

I wanted to become an agent because I became intrigued with it and the process behind it. More importantly, I believed that everybody has a beauty—something about them that's unique. We're all different colors and races with different creeds. I might jump rope, but you can double dutch; you get me?

People don't know that at the age of six, I got hit by a car. The story that I'm told was that it was a drunk driver who ran a red light and hit me as I was walking home from school. I literally went up in the air and when I came down, I hit the hood of the car and held on because they didn't realize what they had done. I was left with scars on my right arm and the back of my right thigh. People don't really pay close attention to them, but they're there.

I'm 60 years old and African American. Back in "the day," when I started modeling with Alan Benfield Bush,

I was shocked. It was still the climate where you had to be pencil thin, blonde-haired, blue-eyed, with a thin face, and I just never saw that as attractive. I think we're all unique and special in our own way, and I didn't believe what I was being told. I didn't believe in the standard of modeling back then.

People would tell me all these reasons why I couldn't do it. When I wanted to model, meeting Alan was a blessing for me because he told me to forget about it, that what they said didn't matter. I'm not afraid to step outside of the box and celebrate everyone's beauty, everyone's uniqueness.

I don't aspire to be like the Creative Arts Agency (CAA), the William Morris Agency (WMA), or the Gersh Agency. I like being a small boutique agency because it has that intimate, family kind of vibe to it. I don't want to be at a point where I'm disconnected from people so much. I try to do and be the person who I want people to be for me. It doesn't matter where you come from; I don't care about that, just be true to yourself and true to me.

Phil Sullivan
Model, America's Next Top Model Contestant

There is no time limit for a male model. I know guys who are sixty years old and they're beautiful and it's unbelievable. When I had just started in the entertainment industry, I knew I would always have opportunities. Whether or not it was something I want to continue to do, is another story. I'm not worried about that for the rest of my career, but there is still that anxiety about what I can do to take advantage of this.

I feel I have to make an impact, and it's a lot of pressure, to be honest with you. You end up going in circles a lot, knowing you want to make a difference, but not knowing how you make that difference. So, you try to dip your hands into everything and just create a better overall dynamic.

It's unbelievable how much the industry relies on networking. I mean, I don't "party." It's actually one of the negatives of my career. I wish I had more of a capacity to party, to network, to end up wherever, be on a plane, be in a club, be in whoever's room however late. I don't have it in me. I've tried. It's not for me.

Everyone who knows me, knows I'm going to be upstate on the weekend. I'm going to be hiking. I'm going to be checking out the stores at ten o'clock. Most people are going to be dancing at 5 am at some crazy event. I lose out on jobs 100% because of that, but I also choose that. You can get lost in a crowd, too, and you might not want to be around those people. Certain choices can impact your life and you have to be careful of your reputation.

It's great to be a role model and I love it when people ask me to tell them what I know. It's because I wish that I'd had a mentor when I went through all this. I really didn't. I will gladly give anybody in the industry advice if I can help.

From the beginning of my career, I've nailed it. Everyone's got these expectations, and it's funny because I'm exceeding them just because I pushed through and climbed even higher!

However, at the same time, it is frustrating. I know to some extent I'm lucky. I've been very fortunate to have my family support me and my career because there are times when I'll have no money and then I'll have a bunch of money. It's one of those weird things. I guess the main focus, I think, with Top Model, is maintaining your integrity and being real, being raw, being vulnerable, and being okay with that.

There is something that can be said about being rejected.

CHAPTER 8 - LOOKING AT SUCCESS

The thing about being rejected is that it pushes you. It makes you want to be better and strive for more. If someone tells you that you can't do something, you have more of a drive to prove them wrong. So, try to figure it out and ask how you can play to your strengths.

If you love it, keep doing it, and don't live by other people's expectations. I think that's one of the biggest things. When you start living by somebody else's expectations, you're almost eliminating your dream. I can't be you. I can't do that. This is what I'm good at and this is what I'm going to do, and no one else has to appreciate that but me.

Santino Fontana
Tony-Award Winning Actor, Voice of Prince Hans (Frozen, 2013), TV Actor, Broadway Actor

You have to be able to remind yourself that what you love to do has to outweigh all the crap, and there really is a lot of crap.

Not only is it hard to deal with the rejection, but there's also no real sense of security in what you do. It's that there is a lot of crap to deal with, but if you can balance that out with a positive mindset, looking at the brighter side of things, then it's all worth it.

It's always about checking in with yourself about what's feeding you at the moment. Think of it like playing the game "The Floor is Lava" when you were a kid. You're jumping around, navigating the furniture, and trying to avoid the floor because it's "lava." You're trying to choose the best path to make sure you don't fall; and it's a surprisingly similar experience navigating the entertainment industry. It's building the instinct of knowing where the lava is and where is safe. At its core, that's what the industry is. If you can reroute my thinking into yours for any show or any audition, then you're going to be fine, and that's kind of what makes it fun.

You also usually end up doing different things, and I think that's also what makes it fun. I think that outweighs all the other stuff. I think it's important to not put pressure on yourself. Don't give yourself a timeline. Give yourself space. There's no rush and there's also no finish line. As they say, "It's a marathon; it's not a sprint."

Also, remember that it's not logical. Don't try to find reason in something that can be random. I've been a reader in auditions where people have come in and I thought they were brilliant. But the director or the casting didn't like them for something silly, like the person reminded them of a friend they had a recent falling out with or that they reminded them of an aunt they don't like. Sometimes it really doesn't make sense.

Just remember what you can control and what you can't control. *There's no point in worrying about things you can control because you can control them and there's no point in worrying about things you can't control because you can't control them.* So, just focus on you—what you do and what you love to do, and that's it.

Jesse Heiman
Actor, The World's Greatest Extra

I'm really happy with my progress. I remember when I first came to L.A.; I had a few set goals, like things that I wanted to accomplish so that I could look back and say that I made good choices and that I was glad that I made the move.

I wanted to be able to say that I had made it. One of those things that I said that I wanted to do was to try to work with Steven Spielberg. It sounds like a really crazy ambition, but within a year and a half of moving to L.A., I was working with Stephen Spielberg on *Catch Me If You Can.*

In the very last scene, of course, Leonardo DiCaprio is pretending to be a substitute teacher. There was a point during the filming when he came up to me and talked with me. That was really cool. Then Spielberg came right up to me and addressed me personally, too, which was just amazing. To get any direction from him, just to get an acknowledgment that I existed in his world, was amazing. So, within a year and a half, I made my dreams come true, and I decided, well, this is it. I'm an actor.

I would definitely say relationship-building is very important as an actor. One of the best relationships I've ever had to this day was with my second agency. I was with my original agency for around a year and a half. Then they signed a guy named Shia LaBeouf and said they didn't need me because they had him. So, then I got some jobs, and I looked for a new agency. My second agency was one of the ones that responded first. They said they were excited to have me, and I was just hooked.

I have been with them since I started in film. They're the best tool in my pocket. They know exactly how to market me, what parts to send me in for, and what parts I'll automatically book—like, as soon as I walk in the room—I'm the guy.

This is one of my tips for anyone becoming an actor: you only need one set of people to believe in you, whether that is an agent, a manager, or a publicist. It's someone that you trust to always have your back. For me, it was that agency. For others, it's a manager, or it's a publicist. If you have that person who believes in you and you believe in yourself as much as you can, you can accomplish anything in this town, anything you want.

You need to believe in yourself because it's not just about luck or all these famous connections you make. The best connection you can make is with one group of people that really believes in you. Everything they've submitted me for has been really exciting. I've done amazing things, some really passionate projects that I'm proud of and even small roles that I'm proud of.

People take luck for granted, thinking it just happens. I feel like everything that happens, happens for a reason and everything works out for you in some way. Even if the thing that you're trying so hard to book doesn't come through, you can be picked for a supporting role in something else coming up the next day and you'll be set.

You shouldn't take any size role for granted. Anything that you can sink your teeth into as an actor and really focus on as a performer will be a great thing for you. Every time a new challenge presents itself, I'm excited. Excited to take on that challenge and that's what keeps me going: just knowing that every day is a new challenge.

You can overcome anything in any line of work. It's not just acting. This could apply to any job or career. What drives me is knowing that what I'm doing is worthwhile. It doesn't matter how long or how hard you go for it. If you put in that hard work, you'll have something great as the result.

There is a lot of downtime in this business, a lot of waiting at home, waiting for the next thing. There are times you've been on a roll, but then there is always the quiet low of nothing going on. You have to understand it's nothing about you. The industry is very seasonal. It has ups and downs too. You have to be able to take every bump in the road and just roll with it.

It's something that you get used to. I used to always be able to fall back on extra work; go back to my roots and start over again or go take some more classes.

I've taken improv and done different types of classes, and it all helps. It all adds up and helps you in your career, so take advantage of it. When I have downtime, I take advantage of it to go see my parents, go see family, and maybe go on a trip. I would tell anyone who's out there trying to get started or just getting started to hang in there. If you're struggling, don't worry about it. We all struggled. You'll find your way and it'll be amazing.

Scott Patrick Erwin
Actor, Model, Writer

We are in 2023. When I started on this journey, it was 2019, and I was in a pretty dark place mentally. Life was sort of crashing around me, and I chose to turn towards myself and ask, "how do I save myself in this lifetime?" It took a while to do but choosing to do something that I enjoy, that I find pleasure in, and that I think I have some relative talent in, has been so satisfying for me.

It wasn't the first period I've had like that, but it was the darkest, deepest one I've had so far. Not that I want another one, but it's really a choice, to choose yourself and choose those things that are going to fill you up instead of break you down.

To me, the society that we have isn't conducive to helping calm our nervous system and our minds. To find that place of peace and balance, you have to be very specific about wanting to do it. That was part of my process: rebooting myself as a creative. That helped me to find value in myself to keep moving forward to reach that place.

In the beginning, I had a mindset coach, and we did a bunch of different techniques: NLP, hypnosis, meditation, things like that. That was during the COVID period. It was around the time I was ready to dive deep into what I wanted to do next. At the same time, I was already doing so many things creatively. I did a lot of writing and worked on my second book. I blogged, and I started a podcast—it was a creative period that set me in this direction. I also found VIP Ignite around that same time.

What came out of that whole period of my life was realizing that I'm not just a cog in the machine of life and society. We all have value and should pursue our dreams to do the things that make us happy. We don't have to be stuck in darkness or depression, overwhelmed, stressed, or anxious. If the career doesn't satisfy you, then damn, choose something else.

It may take a while. It comes in waves. You get through six months and feel great, but then you can go through the next twelve months feeling not so great. It comes in different phases and intensities. It's the cycle of life, but I wasn't going to stay where I was and beat myself up. I was ready to make that choice and take that step in a different direction. I could finally say to myself, "I don't care what I do, but I'm not doing *that* anymore."

Thomas G. Waites
Director, Producer, Writer

I've been sober twenty years as of June 7th, 2023. This is the thing that I am most proud of. I would have gone much further in my career by now had I not been interrupted by the disease of alcoholism, and I blame no one but myself for it. No one asked me to drink. No one ever poured a bottle down my throat. I did it to myself. It was definitely a self-inflicted destruction. Nothing pushed me to drink.

Nothing pushed me to stop, either. Nowadays, my children love and respect me so much. They absolutely spoiled me with their love, but it wasn't like that when I was drinking. They didn't want to talk to me, and they completely detached themselves from me. It hurt, but it didn't hurt enough to make me stop. What *did* hurt enough was the possible loss of the love and friendship of my ex-wife, Lisa Greenberg.

We weren't together romantically anymore; we had gone through the divorce, but we were still close friends. She came to me and threatened to withdraw. She said that she didn't want to be my friend anymore. She said that if I continued the way I was going, she'd refuse to be my friend.

Here's a woman who feeds the homeless every Friday when she's in New York. Here's a woman who went to Africa to feed and aid impoverished children. This is a woman who would and does love everyone with all her heart, and yet, she did not want to be my friend because I was a drunk.

That was what broke the camel's back. I'd lost her love long ago. I already drank that away, but I couldn't lose her friendship.

It really brings everything full circle. Relationships. They can open your career, keep your career, and even save your life. Lisa saved my life. She is the hero of this story. She is the reason for my success. I mean, I have so much going for me now: I've written and directed my own feature film; I have a rock & roll band which is awesome; I've written my own music that's to be featured in my film; I even have a very successful acting studio that I'm going to have to start a waiting list for. It's crazy. I have a great life now.

And that's something you can't tell an addict. Whether it's alcohol or drugs, you just can't say to them, "Hey, if you get to the other side of the mountain, it's great over there. Things get so much better if you just make that climb." But because we're so self-absorbed we wouldn't hear you.

Addiction is a very selfish disease. It's destroyed many, many families, and many careers. There are so many people who wish they'd put it down sooner. I wish I'd put it down sooner, but eventually, I did. I did it with the right help from the right person, and I cannot thank her enough.

Les Brown

Motivational Speaker, Politician, Former Ohio State Representative

T.D. Jakes said something that I truly believe: "Success is not success without a successor." I turned seventy-eight this year, and so now I am looking for my successors from a small group of people who I can pass the torch to.

I have some years behind me and hopefully some more before me, but there will come a time when I'm no longer here, just like all the others before me. In 1992, the top five speakers in the world were: General Norman Schwarzkopf, Robert Schuller, Paul Harvey, Leon Coker, and me. Now all the other four are gone. I'm still here and my number is going to come up, but before I leave, I am going to make an impact.

I am going to empower speakers and teach them how to use their stories to speak to a world that will get to see a future that I won't get to see. I'm teaching them how to transform an audience and create an experience with their story to distract, dispute, and inspire people toward change. They can dismantle the belief systems of the people who listen to them and build them back up to allow them to begin that new chapter of their lives.

It's something, a change, that I won't get to see. But I will be present with them with my spirit. We can actually leave a legacy that can be preserved long after we're gone. Each person is a masterpiece because they are a piece of the master.

~~~~~~~~~~~

CONCLUSION

If you had the opportunity to hone your craft, build your skill set, and the opportunity to connect with all these people, why wouldn't you?

Why wouldn't you want to . . .

- hear from some of the greats about how they got to become great?

- be face-to-face with Academy Award-winning directors?

- talk directly to some of the best casting agents and talent agents in the industry?

- have your music or your voice heard by major record labels?

- work with some of the biggest brands to help launch your modeling career?

So, if you had the chance to succeed in the entertainment industry, would you take it? I asked you that at the beginning of this book. Have you decided?

VIP Ignite is here to help you understand the industry you're in, to give you some guidance on which paths to take, and to open so many more doors than you thought was even possible through the power of connections.

There is so much about this industry that people just don't know. They will probably never know more than half of the story. The likelihood is you'll know all about blockbuster films, chart-topping albums, the next big thing from the next big brand, or even the latest scandal. What you won't know is the day-to-day of all those who aren't making the headlines, and sometimes even those who are because it goes unseen and unknown.

So, if you're stepping into this industry, if you're struggling in this industry, or if you're aspiring to be in this industry, know that being here is not impossible.

Everyone who is successful has put in the work, time, and time again. They've taken chances and expanded their resumes, but most importantly, they've built relationships that people remember. Everything they have done has given them the ability to connect with someone helpful to them, whether that be with a job or simply an opportunity to learn. They have been able to navigate those roadblocks and obstacles because they've had people there to guide and support them.

We want to be there to support you, to give you control over the career you want to have, but also to be there to build you up. We want to be there, giving you everything you need to stand out and stand up on your own two feet. Working in this industry is hard, but it's not difficult if you stay patient, persistent, and passionate with the right people behind you.

WHAT ARE YOUR NEXT STEPS?

You can apply to become part of our talent now.
VIPIGNITELIVE - How to Start Your Modeling and Acting
Career https://vipignitelive.com/

Due to the high level of our speakers and industry experts, we are only able to work with a small amount of talent at any given time. We have limited spots available due to the number of people who apply daily. If we feel this is not the right moment for you, you'll be added to a one-year waiting list. Don't worry, we won't forget about you. Our reasons for this are to give you the amount of time we think is necessary to improve your skill set and to get your life organized professionally, financially, and emotionally.

By getting started now, you will have the opportunity to meet with casting directors, producers, and agents who are casting immediately. The best time to plant a tree was twenty years ago, but the next best time is today. People who push past that roadblock and who take the leap are more likely to succeed. Those who take massive action get massive results. By acting now, it shows you are motivated and in momentum and at the end of the day, that is what the entertainment industry looks for in people.

Our offer is a complete program and experience that includes everything needed to start or grow a career as a model, actor, or musician. This is what you are will get:

1. **Live photo shoots** throughout the year in various locations in the continental United States. These shoots

WHAT ARE YOUR NEXT STEPS?

include celebrity photographers, makeup artists, and stylists. We bring in the best people because this not only gives you the first tools you need, which are great photos used for press kits, portfolios, and headshots, but more importantly, it gives you a leg up on your resume by working with industry legends. These photographers, makeup artists, and stylists can instantaneously change the trajectory of your life just by sharing your photos on their social media, thus giving you exposure to an exponentially growing list of brands and clients that they work with daily.

2. **VIP 30X Elite Academy**. This is an online, live training done weekly throughout the year and is hosted by a variety of industry experts, who can be television and film stars who have worked with such directors as Martin Scorsese, Francis Ford Coppola, Oliver Stone, and others. You also get to work with the heads of major modeling agencies ranging from Ford to IMG and Wilhelmina Models, to name a few. These individuals are all currently working and are successful at the highest level. And, as a talent, you are getting inside access to decades of knowledge weekly, live, and online. These training sessions are also networking opportunities since they are all working individuals—casting directors, managers, magazine publishers, and a plethora of industry insiders who are all looking to hire new talent.

3. **Live training sessions** are consistently going live. We have over 400 hours of content that we archived in our **VIP Vault** that is searchable by keyword where you can access it twenty-four hours a day, seven days a week. This one-of-a-kind archive has some of the most incredible

content and training and is not available anywhere else in the world. Training includes such notables as the current Phantom of the Opera on Broadway, the founder of Ford Models, and the head of casting for L'Oréal, Gap, and Banana Republic. We even include training from leaders in business, finance, and mindset. Such notables include Dragan Trajkovski, Laura Sicola, Roxanne Messina Captor, and Brandon Steiner. We do this because we believe that becoming successful in life is not only about creativity, but also about the right mindset, business acumen, knowledge of health and relationships, and an overall understanding of the tools and keys to success.

4. **We provide specialized training** dealing with current trends and important knowledge that you need to utilize right now, from managing your online presence to understanding where the industry is heading. Examples include Social Media Domination, Streaming Services, Fashion Trends, Industry Forecasts, Relationship Building, Networking, and Millionaire Mindset.

5. **We provide access to live and/or virtual events** where you have the opportunity to sit down and meet with over thirty-five of the most influential and powerful people in the entertainment industry. These are the individuals who created the brands, shows, and films that have influenced generations. This is your opportunity, face to face, to meet the people who can snap their fingers and change your lives in thirty seconds or less. Our offer makes your life better because it's a perfect offer. It includes everything that you need to get started or elevate your career. You no longer have to worry or live in fear that you don't have the right connections, guidance, or

influence to accelerate both your life and career. We have vetted, done all the research, and brought you the best of the best in the world, people you would never have access to at this stage in your career. This in turn allows you to not only have the knowledge and connections you need to succeed but also enables you to unlock the roadmap that you can follow that has proven results and takes your life from being ordinary to extraordinary.

6. **Speaker's Bureau.** We've added a speaker's division where we've started to reach out to people outside the entertainment industry—entrepreneurs, writers, financiers, and others who will help you to excel in all areas of your life and career, not just when you're on stage or in front of a camera. A lot of big companies have the money to bring in these people for their own employees to improve their knowledge and skills, so why can't we do the same for our talent?

7. **Truth Management.** This is something we've spoken about a little bit in this book, but you'll have the opportunity to be a part of this international database for talent. It has state-of-the-art automation for production companies of all sizes and is a dominant force for giving you control of your career while negotiating better rates on your behalf.

TESTIMONIALS

"I've been working as an actor for several years now, and one of the struggles I've had is getting the roles, the call-backs, and getting the auditions. I was stuck. At every audition, I did the same thing over and over again, expecting a different result. So, I decided I was going to stop the cycle. I was going to look for someone who could give me the opportunities to make those connections that drive the relationships in this industry. The connections that would get me to where I need and want to be. VIP Ignite was that someone.

They don't make promises they can't deliver. They are the real deal. When they talk the talk, they can walk the walk. And to me, that's what is important. They give you the tools, the connections, and the opportunities to accelerate your career.

Through VIP Ignite, I've been able to sit down with talent and talent agents 1:1 to talk about the industry, to show them my resume and headshots, and to hear that they want to work with me. Michael, Alycia, Deneen, and VIP Ignite made that happen. They've helped me get to the right place with the right people. That's mind blowing!"

— **Andrea "Andi" Matusiak,** *actor*

"VIP Ignite reached out to me and put me in a room with people who are successful in all areas of the industry. So, it was a no-brainer to try getting closer and to work with them. Whether or not my journey ended there, I was going to get an education from people who are already successful, doing what I want to do.

Instead of having to do the legwork of trial and error and not really knowing how, I wasn't alone. It's amazing to have so many prominent figures coaching me and working with me all in one place. Regardless of whether it's acting or entertainment, connections are everything. You can't do it on your own and VIP Ignite gives you that network so you can jump in and build those relationships that help you invest in yourself and in your career."

— Heather Prescott, *musician, singer/songwriter*

"I have been with VIP Ignite for just over a year, and I'm so glad I'm with them. It is a big family and the whole team is so phenomenal. With every event I go to, they just get greater and greater. You never know what you're going to get out of it, but it's constant growth. I love it, and now, I know I'm going somewhere!"

— Zandra Sterling, *actor, voice actor, model, writer*

"The reason I'm part of VIP Ignite's Inner Circle is simple: I want to be successful. You can chase your dream, but if you don't have all the tools to do it, you're not going to get very far. I've spent 40+ years in the music industry and I did okay, but I wasn't what I would call successful. I was stuck and was looking for something else. Everything I found turned out okay, but I wanted more than okay, and that led me to VIP Ignite and the Inner Circle.

It took me a long time to figure out that I needed more than just me. I needed the tools and the team; I needed people to work with me and guide me, to tell me what I'm doing right and what I'm doing wrong. And now I have all these people with VIP Ignite who can help me but also who I can help in return."

— **Mike "Trash" Betchel,** *musician, actor*

"VIP Ignite is amazing. In my life, they have delivered—consistently; everything they said they would do for me, they have done. I have been put in front of people who have seen my talent; I have been able to ask the right questions to the right people. I have been able to extend my connections and through their support and the opportunities they offer, I have grown more confident in my talent and skills. With VIP Ignite I am more prepared than I have been in a long time, and it's only going to go forward."

— **David Drumgold,** *actor, writer, producer*

"VIP Ignite and Truth Management will put you into the arena that you need to be in when you're serious about being and working in the entertainment business. You grow and develop not only professionally but in your personal life as well.

By trusting in the process and doing the work with VIP Ignite's wonderful coaches and training, I have been able to take my journey to the next level. With everything that VIP Ignite offers, you have an abundance of resources at your fingertips to learn from and excel. You have their events and workshops, their Zoom calls and office hours, and even through the Vault, a digital library which has everything you need to explore and enhance your skills.

No matter what level you have in this industry, from the experienced to the inexperienced, you have to keep growing and you can grow to your full potential with VIP Ignite."

— Cyd Sana Rasool, *actor, model*

"I started my journey with VIP Ignite, with their online classes and learning how I could get my foot in the door. They gave me all the tools, education, and support I needed to push my career further. They give you so many connections with real people who are active in the industry, from young to old and in all areas of the entertainment industry. It's unreal. No matter what field you want to go into, they'll be able to connect you with the right people at the right time to get you to where you want to be."

— Wendy Fout, *actor, model, writer*

"Before VIP Ignite, my journey was going down a very winding road filled with potholes and traps. I was worried about my direction, but with VIP Ignite, I have been able to differentiate truth from fiction and I have found the direction I need to go to get where I want to be. And if I ever have a question, I know all I have to do is pick up the phone and give them a call.

VIP Ignite gives you the support and real industry guidance you need if you want to work in this industry; they're not going to give you the BS and they have your back 110%."

— Marsa Clark, *commercial actor and model*

"Before VIP Ignite, my career, my journey was going at a snail's pace, but it was the people that finalized my decision to join them. I'm not a sugar person, I'm not a fluff person; if somebody's telling me, "Yes, you can be in this business," but they're not giving me the real deal, then that's a red flag for me. With VIP Ignite, I just knew that these were the people to point me in the right direction. They tell you the truth.

Since joining, the big difference in my career is the kind of interactions I'm having. With VIP Ignite, I'm having interactions with the *real* people in the *real* business. I'm not interacting with someone else's opinions or dreams, but with the people who are already there. I get to ask them the real questions that I need answers to, to be able to excel in this industry.

With VIP Ignite, I'm in the right spot at the right time."

— **Ada Cruz,** *voice actor, actor, commercial model, writer*

"I believe in VIP Ignite and I trust that they are leading me in the right direction. From day one when I got on the Zoom call there were major connections that I never would have gotten on my own. As a musician, I tried to reach out on my own and I got a little bit, but I have gotten so much more with VIP Ignite. They lift you up and allow you to grow your skills and confidence by giving you access to those top-level connections that you otherwise wouldn't have—unless you were already something in the industry."

— **Tony Aguilera,** *singer/songwriter, actor*

"There is no better place to be than with VIP Ignite. As an actor, you won't have a job without networking, without being in the right place and with the right people. VIP Ignite gives you the opportunities to build those relationships that you need to have to get where you want to be.

Before VIP Ignite, I was lost. I was on the right path, but I didn't have a clue what I was doing. Then I found Alycia and VIP Ignite, and everything fell into place. I started going to events and boot camps, and I found my tribe with VIP Ignite. You can't do it alone and you can't do it with the wrong people. You need the right people and when you have the right people, they will give you everything you need to keep going and find success in this industry."

— **Noreen Belz,** *actor*

"My experience with VIP Ignite was life changing. I never knew what to expect whenever I got to one of their events. But I always knew that I'm going to have some great opportunities, partake in some amazing activities, network with talent, directors, and casting agents, and be able to put myself out there.

Thanks to VIP Ignite, I got to improv with Thomas G. Waites at one of their events, which was incredible. I showed up as my most authentic self and I asked him a simple question; I connected with him through music. Even now, I have no words to describe it; I'm still amazed it happened.

Even though I may not know what is happening between these meetings, moments, and connections, what is happening here is opening up doors and pathways that I can't even imagine. VIP Ignite makes a lifetime of difference."

— **Candyce Raiford,** *musician, actor, model, production*

"VIP Ignite is pretty serious about helping people in the entertainment industry. They want nothing but to push you through the doors with everything you need to find success.

The experiences I've had with VIP Ignite are surreal. I have been able to meet with agents and talent scouts and talk with them 1:1 about what they do and what I do, and they were *real* people in the industry. VIP Ignite puts you in front of real people who have *real* credentials, experience, and success, then supports you in making those *real* connections that are going to help you succeed in this industry."

— **Wesley Poss,** *actor, singer, model*

"I've been with VIP Ignite for four years, and before I joined them, my career wasn't moving at the speed or pace that I was expecting it to. It got to the point where I was so close to just saying, "I guess this just isn't for me," and then I found VIP Ignite. Within the first day, they rekindled my desire, and they gave me hope that I can become a successful working actor.

The beautiful thing with VIP Ignite is they're brutally honest. They're not going to sugarcoat it. They're not guaranteeing that they can make you a star; they are guaranteeing that you are starting your journey with the right people and the right connections so that you can make it happen. What they do is find the keys to the door and unlock it, but you still have to take that step through. They give you the opportunities that you wouldn't have on a normal, average day."

— **Karl Licht,** *actor*

"VIP Ignite brings together people from all walks of life and experience. They are there to give you the best knowledge possible, to bring out the best in you as an artist. They help you navigate this industry and connect with some of the most important people that can really push your career to the next level. They allow you to network with them 1:1 and get into their minds to find out how they got to where they are and see where you could possibly be going next.

With VIP Ignite, I have made some phenomenal connections. I speak to people every day who I never even thought I'd be in a room with, and it's amazing to me because it shows me how far I've grown but also that I'm with the right team. On so many levels, it's amazing.

VIP Ignite has changed my life. I am forever filled with joy and gratitude because of VIP Ignite. I say that because they have changed me for the best."

— **Leslie Pena,** *actor, model*

"One of the things that people don't get a whole lot of throughout the entertainment journey, is mentorship. If you're lucky, you might have a couple people who have been in the industry longer than you, who will impart gems of wisdom and lessons that they've learned along the way, but it's kind of rare. And if you're just getting started and you don't have a huge resume behind you, sometimes you're stepping into the unknown.

So, the best thing you can do is reach out. VIP Ignite is going to be a great resource for you. It is a community of people who are taking control of their own lives and careers, and who are wanting to learn and apply the knowledge that people like me share with them—whether that is just my story or the mistakes I've made along the way. It's that community that VIP Ignite fosters that separates it from anything else out there. Through working with them, you will embrace your authenticity, elevate your performance, and get the jobs you always wanted."

— **Jai Rodriguez,** *actor, Broadway actor, TV actor*

ABOUT THE AUTHOR

Michael Fomkin, the Connection King, has dedicated almost two decades to helping models, actors, and musicians connect with the most influential people in the industry through VIP Ignite. He is one of the top experts in the industry and is the founder of Truth Management, the fastest-growing talent management firm in the USA. He recently expanded his horizons to represent individuals who have something to say and merely need a stage to speak from.

He set himself the goal to change the perspectives of the entertainment industry for the people who are unique and who are different, to help them connect and succeed in this industry. In doing so, he has invested over a million dollars in education and leadership and has spoken live and virtually from some of the world's biggest stages. He is also a Broadway Investor, forever supporting the arts.

Michael has won over thirty-eight awards throughout his career and recently added another accolade to his collection:

The Lifetime Achievement Award 2022 for his contributions to the Media and the Entertainment Industry.

His company frequently donates to Operation Underground Railroad, helping free over 3,500 kids worldwide from sex trafficking, and has helped with the cause of eradicating homelessness in multiple cities.

When he's not pouring himself into his work, he often takes the time to indulge in his love of baseball or relaxes with a game of MTG, Magic: The Gathering.

Made in the USA
Middletown, DE
21 October 2023

41163618R00126